MAKE YOUR OWN
SOFT TOYS

MAKE YOUR OWN
SOFT TOYS
GAIL ATTWELL

Photography by Janek Szymanowski

NEW HOLLAND

First published in the UK in 1991 by
New Holland (Publishers) Ltd
37 Connaught Street, London W2 2AZ

Reprinted in 1992 and 1993

ISBN 1 85368 158 X (hbk)
ISBN 1 85368 204 7 (pbk)

Editor: Nune Jende
Designers: Janice Evans, Joan Sutton and Tracey Carstens
Cover design: Tracey Carstens
Illustrator: Gail Attwell
Photographer: Janek Szymanowski
Styling and stencilling: Penny Swift
Phototypeset by BellSet
Originated by Unifoto (Pty) Ltd
Printed and bound in Singapore by Tien Wah Press (Pte) Ltd

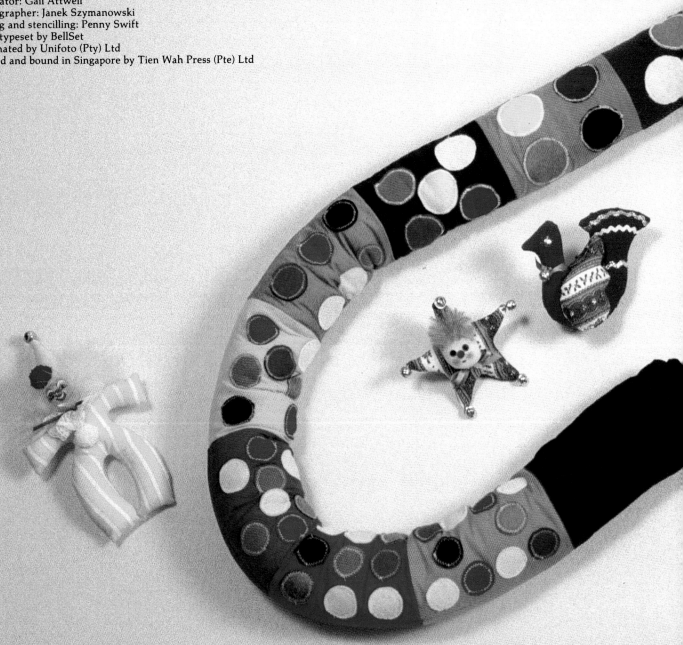

Contents

Before You Start – Hints To Help You

STUFFING

This comes in many different forms and qualities. After all the care you've taken in making the toy, it would be a pity to stuff it with a cheap material that would give it a lumpy appearance. Foam chips, besides being unsafe, are unsuitable, as is kapok, as neither material can be washed. White polyester makes the best quality stuffing.

Use small amounts of stuffing at a time, continually feeling the outside of the toy to ensure that it is smooth and the stuffing is even. To fill small spaces, push tiny bits of stuffing into position, using the blunt end of a crochet hook (a knitting needle is too sharp).

The most important area to stuff properly is the neck. Stuff the neck firmly, otherwise the head will wobble.

COLOUR

Choose colours with care. If making a toy as a decorative feature, match fabrics already in the room, for example, those of the duvet cover, curtains and so on.

Contrasting colours and patterns work well – combine purple or lilac with yellow tones, or apricot and orange with blue tones.

GLUE

A glue gun is a wonderful investment – it has many uses in the home besides toy making. Colourless glue in a tube is also suitable, as it creates a neat appearance.

FABRIC

Preferably use new fabric when making toys, for a crisp, fresh look.

Fabric for bodies and heads can vary. Fine, brushed nylon is recommended, using the wrong side as the right side. The fabric has some stretch, is a good base on which to embroider, paint or glue a face, and is available in a lovely peach colour which gives a realistic flesh tone.

When sewing body pieces together, use a stretch stitch, so set your sewing machine on to a very slight zig-zag stitch.

For clothing, use fabric suitable for the type of toy being made.

FUR FABRIC

This is easy to work with once you know how and is wonderful for hiding less than perfect stitching! First check that your sewing machine can cope with sewing through the thickness.

Always trace the pattern onto the back of the fabric, with the pile of the fur in the direction indicated on the pattern.

Flip over the pattern piece when you have to cut a left and a right piece.

Cut only one thickness at a time, snipping through the woven back of the fabric to avoid cutting through the pile.

After sewing a fur piece, be extra-careful to remove all pins and after turning through the fabric, check for any pile caught in the seams. If necessary, gently run the point of a pin or needle over the seam to release the pile.

When glueing on features such as eyes, trim pile away from the area first.

HAIR

Double knitting wool or 4-ply is the most suitable, and wool with a brushed effect looks good.

1. *For sew-on curls*, wind the wool round as many fingers as necessary to give the required length of a curl.

2. Wind the wool round your fingers as many times as necessary to give the desired thickness of a curl.

3. Cut off the wool, slip the curl off your fingers and stitch twice through the loops of the wool to the head of the toy.

4. Pull the stitches tight and sew the curls next to each other on the head, as close as desired. The curls are normally longer at the back and sides and shorter at the front of the head.

1. *To make strips of curls*, use a length of 6 mm-wide (¼ in-wide) tape.

2. With your sewing machine set on a close stitch, sew a few stitches down the centre of the tape at one end.

3. Wind the wool round your fingers to give the desired length and thickness of curl, remembering that the length of these curls will be half the length you wind round your fingers.

4. Cut the wool, slip the curls off your fingers and position them across the width of the tape. Sew through the middle of the curls.

5. Repeat the procedure of winding the wool round your fingers, sewing the loops closely together until you have a sufficient length of curl-covered tape to make the desired hairstyle.

6. Sew a second row of stitching over the first to strengthen. Sew the tape neatly to the head as required.

7. You can cut through the loops to give a different effect.

ROUGE

Powder rouge, available at any cosmetic counter, is ideal. The rouge does wash out, but is easily touched up.

1. Using the brush provided, start in the centre of the cheek, and brush lightly with a circular motion.

2. Continue adding more rouge until the desired effect is achieved.

NOSES

Stand-out noses are made by cutting a circle of fabric which has some stretch. You can also make a small pompon or glue on a felt nose.

A 7 cm (2¾ in) diameter fabric circle is the usual size unless otherwise stated.

Run a gathering thread round the outer edge. Put a small ball of stuffing into the centre on the wrong side of the fabric, pull up gathers tightly to secure and sew the nose in position.

FELT
Felt is usually bought in squares. Use a good quality felt as the very thin version is not suitable for making shoes or body parts for toys.

When cutting out small pieces of felt, first brush the back of the felt with a little white craft glue and let it dry thoroughly. The glue backing will give small pieces of felt a smooth edge when you cut them out. Bigger pieces of felt should be sewn and not glued onto a toy.

FACES
A beautifully made toy can be spoilt by an ugly face. The less facial detail, the more effective, so don't add too many freckles, eyelashes and so on.

Pin the felt pieces onto the face first, to achieve a pleasing effect. Eyes normally look best if positioned halfway down the face. A sparkle can be added to the eye with a little dot of white felt, or waterproof white paint.

When embroidering facial detail, use three strands of cotton.

THREAD
A strong thread is necessary for certain parts of toy making, especially when pulling up gathers tightly. Ask a haberdasher for advice.

POMPON
The size of each pompon varies depending on the size of the toy. The method is identical for each one: only the diameter of the circles and the amount of wool used will change.

You will need a compass, pencil, pair of scissors, a needle, some wool, cotton thread and thin cardboard.

1. Use a compass to draw two circles with a diameter of the pompon required, on thin card.

2. Cut a hole measuring approximately 8 mm (⅜ in) in diameter in the centre of each circle.

3. Thread a needle with two strands of wool and, holding the two circles together, wind the wool round the circles, passing the needle through the hole each time.

4. Continue winding wool round, cutting off the wool at the outer edge of the circles as it runs out.

5. Rethread the needle with more wool and continue winding in this way until the centre hole is full and the circles are well covered.

6. Snip through the wool, all the way round, between the circles.

7. Slide a length of strong thread between the circles, wind it tightly round the centre a couple of times and tie firmly.

8. Leave the long ends of cotton for attaching the pompons to the toy.

9. Cut the card carefully to the centre and twist the card circles out of the pompon. Fluff out the pompon and trim the ends if necessary.

Baby's First Toys

Both the teddy bear and the bunny are made from the same pattern, except for the ears. Fake fur is not too difficult to work with (see page 6), or you can make these toys from brushed nylon.

REQUIREMENTS

FOR EACH TOY

48 cm x 32 cm (19 in x 12⅝ in) fur.
14 cm x 7 cm (5½ in x 2¾ in) fabric
  for bib.
5 cm x 60 cm (2 in x 23⅝ in) fabric
  for bib binding.
scraps of fabric for inner ears.
squeaker for inside tummy
  (purchased from a craft shop).
felt.
polyester filling.
lace for bib edging.
red embroidery cotton.
glue.
purchased embroidered
  motif (optional).

1. To make the body, transfer the patterns on page 77 onto tracing paper and cut out. Pin the patterns to the fabric and cut out the body front on the fold. Cut out two body backs, four pieces for the arms and two outer ear pieces in fur. Cut out two inner ear pieces in contrasting fabric.

2. With right sides together, sew the body backs, leaving a gap for turning through.

3. With right sides together, sew the arms in pairs, leaving the straight edge open. Turn through and stuff lightly to about 1.5 cm (⅝ in) from the straight edge.

4. With right sides together, sew the inner ears to the outer ears, leaving the straight edge open and turn through.

5. With right sides together, pin and tack the arms and ears to the body front as shown in fig. 1.

6. With right sides together, pin the body back to the body front, enclosing the ears and arms. Sew round the outer edge, thus incorporating the arms and ears into the seam. Leave a gap for turning through

7. Clip into the curves and turn through.

8. Stuff the legs lightly and topstitch across the tops of the legs as indicated on the pattern.

9. Stuff the rest of the body and head, enclosing a squeaker, if desired. Sew the gap closed.

10. Trim the fur pile from the eye and nose positions. Cut the eyes and nose (patterns on page 77) from felt and glue in position. Embroider the mouth.

11. To make the bib, transfer the pattern on page 77 onto tracing paper and cut out. Pin the pattern to the fabric and cut out two bib pieces.

12. With right sides together, tack lace round the outer edge of one bib piece, aligning the straight edges.

13. With right sides together, sew the bib pieces, leaving the straight edge open and turn through.

14. With right sides together, pin the centre of the bib binding to the centre of the bib back. Sew the binding in position across the top of the bib.

15. Fold the binding over to the front of the bib and tuck in the raw edges at each end of the binding as shown in fig. 2.

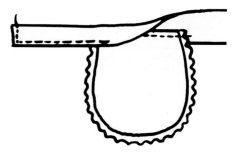

Fig. 2

16. Turn under a small hem along the free edges of the binding and sew along the entire length. Sew a purchased motif onto the bib front, if desired.

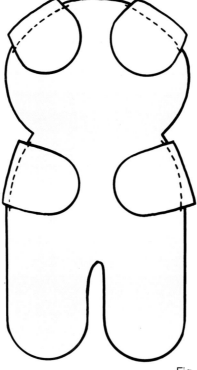

Fig. 1

Novelty Bibs

These bibs are quick and easy to make and the delightful, little toys are attached to the bibs with press studs.
You can sew a loop of elastic onto the back of each toy to make a finger puppet for wonderful dinner-time entertainment!

REQUIREMENTS

FOR THE BIB

30 cm x 56 cm (12 in x 22 in) fabric for upper bib and back.
17 cm x 32 cm (6¾ in x 12⅝ in) contrasting fabric for bottom front.
45 cm x 55 cm (17¾ in x 21⅝ in) iron-on vilene.
85 cm of 2 cm-wide (33½ in of ¾ in-wide) pre-gathered lace.
80 cm of 12 mm-wide (31½ in of ½ in-wide) double fold bias binding.

FOR THE ELEPHANT

44 cm x 17 cm (17⅜ in x 6¾ in) brushed nylon.
scrap of contrasting fabric for inner ears.
polyester filling.
narrow ribbon for round neck.
three transparent press studs.
black embroidery cotton for eyes.
powder rouge.

FOR THE CLOWN

26 cm x 9 cm (10¼ in x 3½ in) fabric for body/arms.
scrap of flesh-coloured fabric for head/neck.
polyester filling.
scrap of pre-gathered lace.
narrow ribbon for round neck.
fake fur for hair.
scrap of felt for hat.
three transparent press studs.
black embroidery cotton for eyes.
red embroidery cotton for mouth.
powder rouge.
pompons or small felt circles.

1. To make the bib, transfer the patterns on pages 66 and 67 onto tracing paper and cut out. Pin the patterns to the fabric and cut out each bib piece.

2. Pin the bib pieces to the vilene and cut out. Iron the vilene, shiny side down, onto the wrong side of each bib piece.

3. With right sides together, sew the bib front bottom to the bib front top. Fold the bib front bottom along the fold line and press. Tack at each side to secure.

4. With right sides together, tack the lace onto the bib front, round the outer edge (not the neck edge).

5. With right sides together, sew the bib back to the bib front round the outer edge, keeping the neck edge open. Turn through and press.

6. Match the centre of the bias binding to the neck centre. Bind the neck edge, folding in the binding ends to neaten. Use the entire length of the binding, thus making tie ends for the bib at the same time.

7. To make the elephant, transfer the patterns on page 67 onto tracing paper and cut out. Pin the patterns to the brushed nylon and cut out the pieces. Cut out the inner ears from contrasting fabric.

8. With right sides together, sew the two front pieces from X to Y as indicated on the pattern. Clip into the curves and turn through, gently pushing the trunk to the right side.

9. Join the elephant's ears in pairs (one outer ear in brushed nylon and one inner ear in contrasting fabric). Turn through.

10. To make the arms, cut two pieces of fabric each measuring 8 cm x 7 cm (3¼ in x 2¾ in), from brushed nylon.

11. Fold the fabric right sides together and stitch as shown in fig. 1. Trim the corners and turn through.

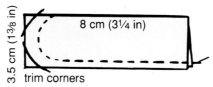

3.5 cm (1⅜ in) | 8 cm (3¼ in)
trim corners

Fig. 1

12. Stuff the arms lightly to 1 cm (⅜ in) from the top.

13. Tack the ears and arms in position as shown in fig. 2.

Fig. 2

14. With right sides together, sew the elephant back to the front, enclosing the arms and ears in the seam and leaving the bottom edge open.

15. Turn through and stuff the head and trunk firmly. Stuff the neck and the body lightly. Turn under a small hem at the bottom edge of the body and sew closed.

16. Run a gathering thread round the neck, pull up the gathers slightly and secure the ends.

17. Using the ribbon, tie a bow round the neck to cover the gathering thread.

18. Sew press studs onto the elephant as shown in fig. 3. Tuck the elephant into the bib pocket and sew press studs onto the bib, aligning them with the press studs on the elephant.

Fig. 3

19. Embroider tiny eyes and rouge the cheeks as described on page 6.

20. To make the clown, transfer the pattern on page 67 onto tracing paper and cut out. Pin the pattern to the fabric and cut out the clown's head/neck. Cut out the body and arms as shown in fig. 4.

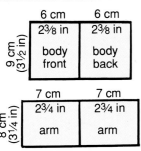

	6 cm	6 cm
9 cm (3½ in)	2⅜ in	2⅜ in
	body front	body back

	7 cm	7 cm
8 cm (3¼ in)	2¾ in	2¾ in
	arm	arm

Fig. 4

21. With right sides together, sew the two head/neck pieces, leaving the bottom edge open. Turn through and stuff.

22. Turn under a small hem at the bottom edge and sew closed.

23. Make the arms as for the elephant, as shown in fig. 1 (see steps 10, 11 and 12).

24. With right sides together, sew the sides of the body, enclosing the arms, as shown in fig. 5. Turn through.

25. Turn under and sew a hem at the top edge of the body and slip the head/neck piece inside. Run a gathering thread round the top edge of the body and pull up the gathers to fit tightly round the clown's neck. Sew the body to the head piece round the neck.

26. Turn under a small hem at the bottom edge of the body and neatly sew closed.

27. Sew the pre-gathered lace round the neck, joining it at the centre back.

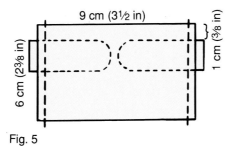

Fig. 5

28. Using the ribbon, tie a bow round the clown's neck. Glue scraps of fake fur for hair round the head.

29. *To make the hat*, transfer the pattern on page 67 onto tracing paper and cut out. Pin the pattern to the felt and cut out the hat.

30. Overlap and glue the straight edges to form a cone. Glue the hat onto the clown's head.

31. Sew on press studs as for the elephant, as shown in fig. 3.

32. Embroider tiny eyes and a mouth, or use waterproof felt-tip pens. Rouge the cheeks as described on page 6.

33. *To make pompons*, follow the instructions on page 7 or cut out circles of felt for the nose and hat decoration.

Hanging Ducks

Make one duck or a whole flock. They look lovely made in bright colours and are wonderful gifts for babies. Attach bells to the cords to add the finishing touch.

REQUIREMENTS
FOR EACH DUCK

two 40 cm x 40 cm (15¾ in x 15¾ in) pieces fabric for body and wings.
scraps of contrasting fabric for beak.
20 cm x 22 cm (7⅞ in x 8⅝ in) of another contrasting fabric for apron.
50 cm x 4 cm (19¾ in x 1½ in) fabric for apron waistband.
felt for eyes.
lace for apron edging.
polyester stuffing.
glue.
bell and ribbon.
black felt-tip pen.
tape or thin cord for hanging.

1. *To make the beak*, transfer the pattern on page 78 onto tracing paper and cut out. With right sides of the beak fabric together, pin the pattern to the fabric. Trace round the pattern and sew the beak, leaving the straight edge open.

2. Cut out the beak, clip into the curves and turn through. Stuff to 1 cm (⅜ in) from the edge.

3. *To make the body*, transfer the patterns on page 78 onto tracing paper and cut out. With right sides of the fabric together, pin the patterns to the fabric and cut out two body pieces, four wings and one gusset.

4. With right sides together, sew the wings in pairs, leaving a gap at the bottom of each wing.

5. Clip into the curves and turn through. Stuff the wings lightly and sew the gap closed. Topstitch round each wing about 6 mm (¼ in) from the edge.

6. Pin the beak to one head piece as shown on the pattern, aligning the edges.

7. Position the cord as indicated on the pattern, ensuring that the long length of cord is to the right side of the fabric.

8. With right sides together, sew the body pieces from A to B as indicated on the pattern, enclosing the beak and the end of the cord into the seam.

9. Sew one side of the gusset to one body bottom edge and sew the other side of the gusset to the other body bottom edge, leaving a gap for turning through.

10. Clip into the curves, turn through and stuff firmly, using small amounts of stuffing. Stuff carefully at the position where the neck flows into the body and sew the gap closed.

11. Glue on the eyes and mark three short eyelashes above each eye with a black felt-tip pen as indicated on the pattern. Sew or glue the wings in position.

12. *To make the apron*, transfer the pattern on page 78 onto tracing paper and cut out. Pin the pattern to the fabric and cut out two apron pieces.

13. Tack lace to the right side of one apron piece, aligning the straight edges.

14. With right sides together, sew the two apron pieces, leaving the straight edge open, and turn through.

15. Run a gathering thread along the top edge of the apron and pull up the gathers slightly.

16. With right sides together, match the centre of the waistband to the centre of the apron and sew the waistband to the apron back. Fold the waistband to the front.

17. Tucking in the raw edges at each side of the tie ends, turn under and sew a small hem along the length of the band to bind the apron top.

18. Thread a bell onto the cord and knot in position. Tie a loop into the top of the hanging cord.

19. Using ribbon, tie a bow above the bell and tie the apron round the duck's neck, below the hanging cord.

Mobile

Use initiative to make any size mobile you desire. Even using a hoola-hoop as a frame proves successful.
This mobile has nine animals, using three basic colours, but the pattern can easily be adapted.

REQUIREMENTS
three 1.2 m (1⅓ yd) lengths of thin
  cane for the frame.
3 m (3¼ yd) of cord for hanging
  (1 m [1 yd 3 in] in each colour).
scraps of fabric for animals.
scraps of felt for ears, tails
  and wings.
black sequins or felt for eyes
  and noses.
1.5 m (60 in) of thin cord or ribbon
  (50 cm [20 in] in each of three
  colours for hanging the animals).
bells and beads for decoration.
felt-tip pens for facial detail.
polyester stuffing.
glue.

7. Clip into the curves and turn through. Stuff each animal body lightly and sew the gaps closed.

8. Glue on the eyes, nose, tail or wings of each animal and add facial details with a felt-tip pen as indicated on the patterns.

9. Using ribbon, tie a bow round the neck of each animal. Sew approximately 15 cm (6 in) of thin cord onto each animal, between the ears of the bunnies and teddies and on top of the ducks' heads.

10. If desired, thread beads and bells onto the cords and knot.

11. Tie the animals evenly round the frame so that it is balanced, securing the knots with glue.

12. Glue or tie a bow at each knot where the cords of the animals are attached to the frame.

1. Make the frame by twisting and joining the three lengths of cane together to form a circle with a diameter of 38 cm (15 in). Mark three points evenly round the frame. At these points tie three equal lengths of cord, with tassles, for suspending the frame. Secure the knots with glue.

2. Tie three short lengths of cord from these points, with tassles hanging down, for decoration.

3. Thread beads or bells onto the short and long cords and knot in position.

4. Tie the three long cords together at the top, forming a loop for hanging the frame.

5. *To make the animals*, transfer the patterns on pages 79 onto tracing paper and cut out. Pin the patterns to the fabric and cut out the teddy, bunny and duck pieces.

6. With right sides together, sew the backs and the fronts, sewing the ears of the bunnies and teddies into the seams as indicated on the patterns. Leave gaps for turning through.

Bride And Bridesmaid

The bride wears a necklace, a garter and carries a horseshoe for good luck, while her bridesmaid carries a cute basket filled with tiny fabric flowers. These dolls make absorbing playmates for young children as the clothes – except the hats – and accessories are removable.
Create your own design for decorating their dresses, using scraps of lace and ribbon.
The dolls are 40 cm (15¾ in) tall. The fabric used for the bodies is cotton knit which has a little more stretch than T-shirt fabric. You may have to experiment to achieve the correct size for the dolls' bodies, but they should measure about 30 cm (12 in) in circumference after stuffing.

REQUIREMENTS
FOR EACH DOLL
75 cm x 25 cm (29½ in x 9⅞ in) cotton knit fabric.
polyester filling.
50 g (1¾ oz) ball of wool is sufficient for three dolls' hair.
strong cotton.
red embroidery cotton for mouth and nose.
scraps of felt for shoes and eyes.
waterproof black felt-tip pen.
powder rouge.
glue.
1 m x 115 cm-wide (1 yd 3 in x 45¼ in-wide) fabric for the dress, hat, pantaloons and petticoat.
5 or 6 mm-wide (¼ in-wide) elastic.
two small press studs.
42 cm x 19 cm (16½ in x 7½ in) tulle or lace for the bride's veil.
lace, ribbon and flowers for decoration.
horseshoe or basket (available from bakeries or bridal shops).

NOTE *Use a 1 cm (⅜ in) seam allowance unless otherwise indicated.*

1. *To make the body,* cut out the fabric as shown in fig.1.

2. With right sides together, fold the body piece in half lengthwise and sew along the length, forming a tube.

3. Run a gathering thread along the top edge of the tube to make the head, using strong cotton. Pull up the gathers tightly and sew the ends securely. Turn through and stuff evenly.

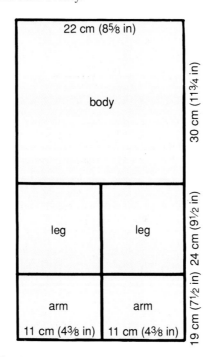

Fig. 1

4. Turn under the bottom edge and sew closed, positioning the seam of the tube at the centre back.

5. *To make the neck,* measure approximately 13 cm (5⅛ in) from the top of the head and tie strong cotton round the tube. Don't pull too tightly or the head will flop. Sew the ends securely.

6. With right sides together, fold each arm and leg piece in half lengthwise and sew as shown in fig. 2.

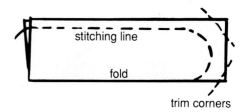

Fig. 2

7. Trim the corners as shown in fig. 2 and turn through. Stuff the arms and legs. The arms should be stuffed to about 4 cm (1½ in) from the top to prevent them being too rigid and should measure approximately 13 cm (5⅛ in) in circumference once stuffed. The legs should measure approximately 14 cm (5½ in) in circumference once stuffed.

8. Turn under the bottom edges of each leg and arm and sew neatly.

9. Sew the arms at shoulder height to the sides of the body, positioning the seams underarm. Sew the legs to the bottom of the body, positioning the seams at the back of the legs.

10. To form the wrists, tie cotton round each arm approximately 4.5 cm (1¾ in) from the end. Sew the ends securely.

11. Embroider the mouth and nose, glue on the eyes and mark the eyelashes with a felt-tip pen as shown in fig. 3. Rouge the cheeks.

Fig. 3   Full-size face

12. *To make the shoes,* transfer the pattern on page 76 onto tracing paper and cut out. Pin the pattern to the felt and cut out a pair of shoes.

13. Sew the shoes as indicated on the pattern, leaving the top edge open, and turn through.

14. Push the doll's feet into the shoes and sew the tops of the shoes round the legs.

15. Tie the ribbon into two small bows and sew onto the front of each shoe.

16. *To make the hair,* follow the instructions on page 6 and wind wool tightly round two fingers for the back of the head (at the neck edge) and round one finger for the sides of the face and the fringe. The number of times you wrap the wool round your fingers depends on the type of wool used and the thickness of the hair required.

17. Slip the wool off your fingers and sew through the loop at one end. Make as many loops as are needed and, starting at centre back, sew the loops round the doll's head.

18. Make a circle of curls round the head, leaving the crown bare since the hat covers it. Trim long ends off hair.

19. *To make the hat,* cut two 30 cm (11¾ in) diameter circles of fabric. With right sides together, sew round the edge of the circles, leaving a gap for turning through.

20. If desired, sew on lace edging.

21. Run a gathering thread round the hat approximately 1.5 cm (⅝ in) from the edge and pull up the gathers so that the hat fits the doll's head, above the circle of curls.

22. Sew the hat onto the head over the gathering stitches, leaving a gap for stuffing. Stuff the hat to create a rounded head and sew the gap closed.

23. *To make the pantaloons,* transfer the pattern on page 77 onto tracing paper and cut out. Pin the pattern to the fabric and cut out two pieces.

24. With right sides together, sew the pantaloons at the centre seams and clip into the curves.

25. Turn under and sew a double hem at the ankle edges of the pantaloons. Sew lace along the edge.

26. Sew tape or ribbon onto the wrong side, just above the ankle hem, to make a casing for the elastic.

27. Thread the elastic through the casing and pull up the elastic to fit snugly round the doll's leg. Tack the ends of the elastic to secure them.

28. Sew the inner leg seams, catching the ends of the elastic in the seams. Clip into the curve at the crotch.

29. Turn under 6 mm (¼ in), then 1 cm (⅜ in) at the waist edge of the pantaloons and press in place. Stitch the waistline hem, leaving a gap to insert elastic.

30. Measure a length of elastic under the doll's arms so that it fits snugly round the doll's body. Thread the elastic through the gap in the hem, overlap the ends of the elastic and sew them securely. Sew the gap closed.

31. *To make the petticoat,* cut a 35 cm x 18 cm (13¾ in x 7 in) strip of fabric. Fold the strip in half widthwise and, with right sides together, sew along the two short edges.

32. Turn under 6 mm (¼ in) and then 1 cm (⅜ in) along one long edge to form a hem. Sew the hem, leaving a gap to insert the elastic.

33. Measure a length of elastic round the doll's waist and thread it through the hem. Overlap the ends of the elastic and sew securely. Sew the gap closed.

34. *To make the petticoat frill,* cut a 110 cm x 8 cm (43⅜ in x 3¼ in) strip of fabric. With right sides together, sew the two short edges. Turn under a double hem at the bottom edge and sew.

35. Run a gathering thread along the top raw edge of the petticoat frill and pull up the gathers to fit evenly round the bottom of the petticoat.

36. With right sides together and matching seams, sew the frill to the petticoat.

37. *To make the dress,* transfer the patterns on page 76 onto tracing paper and cut out. Pin the patterns to the fabric and cut out the pieces.

38. Using lace and ribbon, decorate the bodice front and the sleeves as desired.

39. Join the armhole edges of the sleeves to the bodice front and backs. Clip carefully into the curves, and sew the underarm and side seams.

40. Sew the wrist edges as for the ankle edges (see steps 25, 26 and 27).

41. Turn under a 6 mm (¼ in) hem round the neck edge and tack in position. Sew lace onto the right side of the dress, close to the neck edge.

42. Sew tape or ribbon onto the wrong side, over the raw edge of the neck hem, to form a casing. Thread elastic through the casing and pull it up to fit snugly round the doll's neck. Secure the elastic approximately 1 cm (⅜ in) from each centre back edge.

43. Turn under a double hem along the centre back edges of the bodice and sew.

44. Sew on a press stud at the neck edge and one between the neck and waist.

45. With right sides together, sew the skirt side seams. Turn under and sew a double hem at the bottom of the skirt.

46. Using lace and ribbon, decorate the skirt as desired.

47. Run a gathering thread round the top of the skirt and pull up the gathers evenly to fit the bodice. Matching side seams, sew the skirt to the bodice, overlapping the bodice back edges slightly.

48. *To make the veil,* trim the corners off tulle or lace fabric as shown in fig. 4.

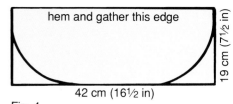

hem and gather this edge

19 cm (7½ in)

42 cm (16½ in)

Fig. 4

49. Measure a length of elastic to fit snugly round the hat. Stretch the elastic and, using a zig-zag stitch on your sewing machine, sew it onto a length of ribbon.

50. Hem the long straight edge of the veil, forming a casing for the elastic-ribbon. Thread the elastic-ribbon through the casing, overlap it and secure the ends.

51. Adjust the gathers in the veil round the back of the head and sew flowers to the front of the ribbon.

52. *To make the garter,* cut a length of ribbon measuring twice the circumference of a leg.

53. Measure a length of elastic to fit snugly round a leg. Using a zig-zag stitch on your sewing machine, stretch the elastic and sew it onto the ribbon.

54. Secure the ends of the elastic-ribbon and sew on a tiny flower or bow.

55. *To make the posy,* cut a 14 cm (5½ in) diameter circle from tulle or lace.

56. Cut a small hole in the centre and run a gathering thread round the hole. Push the stems of flowers through the hole, pull up the gathers tightly and secure.

57. Using ribbon, tie a bow round the stems of the flowers and sew the posy to the doll's hand.

58. *To make the necklace,* use a length of shirring elastic which is long enough to stretch over the hat and head. Thread beads onto the elastic and knot securely.

Olivia Doll

Olivia is 56 cm (22 in) tall. She wears pantaloons and a petticoat under her dress and apron. Trim her clothing with lace and ribbons to match and lace her shoes with narrow ribbon.
An unusual method is used for making her head, which gives a smooth finish to her face. A mohair mix wool for her hair looks wonderful, but any wool with a brushed texture is effective.

REQUIREMENTS
2 m x 50 cm (2¼ yd x 19¾ in) brushed nylon fabric for body and head.
22 cm x 24 cm (8⅝ in x 9½ in) thin wadding.
polyester filling.
a little more than a 50 g (1¾ oz) ball of wool for hair.
1 m x 60 cm (1 yd 3 in x 23⅝ in) fabric for dress.
60 cm x 40 cm (23⅝ in x 15¾ in) fabric for pantaloons.
1 m x 40 cm (1 yd 3 in x 15¾ in) fabric for petticoat and apron.
ribbons of various widths.
3 mm-wide (⅛ in-wide) ribbon for shoe laces.
1 m x 5 cm-wide (1 yd 3 in x 2 in-wide) anglaise-type lace edging for shoulder straps and apron edge.
eyelet anglaise trimming for shoes and dress.
scraps of felt for shoes.
dark pink embroidery cotton.
three press studs.
two 1.5 cm (⅝ in) diameter shanked buttons for eyes.
6 mm-wide (¼ in-wide) elastic.
powder rouge.

1. *To make the head,* transfer the pattern on page 81 onto tracing paper and cut out. Pin the pattern to the fabric and cut out two head pieces.

2. Cut a 22 cm x 24 cm (8⅝ in x 9½ in) piece of brushed nylon fabric. Position the wadding on the wrong (fluffy) side of the brushed nylon fabric and tack.

3. Put one head piece, wrong side down, on top of the wadding. Sew round the outer edge and across the neck edge through all three thicknesses. Cut away the excess fabric and wadding.

4. Mark the features on the head piece as shown in fig. 1. Sew on the eyes, embroider the mouth and nose, working through all thicknesses. Rouge the cheeks.

Fig. 1   Full-size face

5. Cut a strip of brushed nylon fabric for the gusset, approximately 58 cm x 5 cm (22⅞ in x 2 in).

6. With right sides together, sew this strip round the outer edge of the face and neck, easing it round the curves.

7. With right sides together, sew the second head piece to the free edge of the gusset. Turn through and stuff firmly.

8. Run a gathering thread round the neck edge, pull up the gathers tightly and sew the ends securely.

9. *To make the body, arms and legs,* transfer the patterns on page 80 and 81 onto tracing paper and cut out. Pin the patterns to the brushed nylon fabric and cut out the pieces.

10. With right sides together, sew the two body pieces round the outer edge, leaving an 8 cm (3¼ in) gap in the centre of the top (shoulder) seam.

11. Turn through and stuff the body firmly, taking special care to stuff the shoulders very well.

12. Push the neck through the gap in the top seam and pin in position. Sew the head to the body, tucking in more stuffing as needed, using the blunt end of a crochet hook.

13. With right sides together, sew the arms and legs, leaving the top edges open. Clip into the curves, turn through and stuff firmly.

14. Turn raw edges in and sew the arms and legs to the body, in the positions indicated on the pattern by large dots

(the sides of the legs must be in line with the sides of the body.) Sew round twice, to ensure that they are sewn on tightly.

15. ***To make the shoes,*** transfer the pattern on page 81 onto tracing paper and cut out. Pin the pattern to the felt and cut out the shoes.

16. Sew the front seams about 2 cm (¾ in) down from each ankle edge.

17. Using a close zig-zag stitch on your sewing machine, start at centre back seam and sew eyelet anglaise trimming round the right side of each ankle edge, turning under the ends to neaten.

18. With right sides together, sew the rest of the outer seams of the shoes and turn through.

19. Thread narrow ribbon through the anglaise trimming, starting and ending at the centre front of each shoe.

20. Push the doll's feet into the shoes and pull up the ribbon snugly, tying a bow at the front of each shoe.

21. **To make the pantaloons,** transfer the pattern on page 80 onto tracing paper and cut out. Pin the traced pattern to the fabric and cut out the pieces.

22. With right sides together, sew the pantaloons at the centre seams and clip into the curves.

23. Turn under a 6 mm (¼ in) double hem at each ankle edge and sew. Sew narrow lace edging to each ankle edge.

24. With right side together, stitch the inner leg seams, clip into the curves and turn through.

25. Measure a length of elastic to fit snugly round the doll's waist. Turn under an 8 mm (⅜ in) hem at the waist edge, and starting at the centre back, sew the elastic over the raw edge using a zig-zag stitch. Overlap the elastic and sew the ends securely.

26. Measure a length of elastic to fit snugly round each leg. Using a zig-zag stitch, sew the elastic round the inside of each pantaloon leg, approximately 3 cm (1¼ in) up from the lace edge.

27. **To make the petticoat,** cut a 90 cm x 23 cm (35½ in x 9 in) strip of fabric.

28. With right sides together, join the two short edges.

29. Turn under a double hem at one long edge and sew on a lace edging.

30. Turn under 6 mm (¼ in), then 1 cm (⅜ in) along the other long edge to form a casing and stitch in place, leaving a gap in the casing to insert elastic.

31. Measure a length of elastic to fit snugly round the doll's waist and thread it through the casing. Overlap the elastic and sew the ends securely. Sew the gap closed and adjust the gathers evenly.

32. **To make the dress,** transfer the patterns on page 80 and 81 onto tracing paper and cut out. Pin the patterns to the fabric and cut out the pieces.

33. With right sides together, sew along the shoulder seams, joining the front and back bodices, and then bind the neck edge with a length of fabric cut on the cross.

34. Sew a piece of ruffled lace round the neck edge.

35. Turn under and sew a hem at the wrist edge of each sleeve and then sew on lace edging.

36. Run a gathering thread round the top of each sleeve from dot to dot, as indicated on the pattern.

37. Pin the sleeve to the armhole edges of the bodice and pull up the gathers to fit evenly round the armholes. Sew the sleeves to the bodice.

38. Sew the sleeve underarm and the bodice side seams and turn through.

39. Measure a length of elastic to fit snugly round each arm and sew it round the inside of each sleeve approximately 3 cm (1¼ in) up from the wrist edge, using a zig-zag stitch.

40. **To make the skirt,** cut a 92 cm x 26 cm (36¼ in x 10¼ in) piece of fabric.

41. Turn under and sew a hem at the bottom edge of the skirt and sew on lace edging.

42. Run a gathering thread along the top edge of the skirt and pull up the gathers to fit evenly round the bodice of the dress. Sew the skirt to the bodice.

43. With right sides together, sew along the two short edges (back seam) of the skirt, taking a 1.5 cm (⅝ in) seam and stopping about 3 cm (1¼ in) from the waistline.

44. Turn under a double hem at the back edges of the bodice and sew down one side, across the centre back seam and up the other back edge.

45. Sew three press studs down the back of the bodice and sew a bow to the front of the neck.

46. **To make the apron,** cut a 60 cm x 10 cm (23⅝ in x 4 in) strip of fabric and cut the bottom corners as shown in fig. 2.

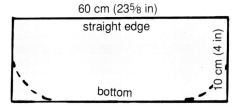

Fig. 2

47. Turn under a small hem and sew anglaise trimming round the sides and bottom edge (from the underside), leaving the straight edge free.

48. Run a gathering thread along the straight edge of the apron, pull up the gathers to measure 30 cm (11¾ in), including the edge of the trimming.

49. Cut a 90 cm x 5 cm (35½ in x 2 in) waistband. Pin the right side of the waistband to the wrong side of the apron, centering it, and sew in position.

50. Turn the waistband to the right side of the apron and turn under a small hem, tucking in the raw edges at each end. Sew along the entire length of the waistband.

51. Measure a length of broad anglaise trimming for each shoulder strap and sew to the inside of the waistband at the back and the front.

52. **To make the plaits,** cut 40 cm (15¾ in) lengths of yarn which, when doubled over, give the thickness for a plait.

53. Tie a piece of strong cotton round the bunch in the centre. Sew the centre of the bunch to the side of the doll's head (at the start of the neck on the side seam).

54. Divide the bunch into three and plait. Secure the ends of each plait with a piece of yarn and decorate using a bow.

55. Follow the instructions on page 6 for making hair. Cover the entire head with short curls, wrapping yarn round two fingers. The method using yarn sewn on tape can also be used.

Baby Bunting

Dressed in her best romper suit made from quilted fabric, Baby Bunting has a face only a mother could love. She is soft and cuddly for a child to sleep with and yet sits neatly on the bed. She is 58 cm (23 in) tall.
For a more personal touch, embroider your child's name on Baby Bunting's bib.

REQUIREMENTS
28 cm x 70 cm (11 in x 27⅝ in)
  flesh-coloured brushed nylon
  fabric for head and hands.
150 cm x 50 cm (59 in x 19¾ in)
  quilted fabric for body, arms, legs
  and bonnet.
two 18 cm x 19 cm (7 in x 7½ in)
  pieces contrasting fabric for bib.
82 cm (32¼ in) bias binding for
  neck of bib and tie ends.
polyester filling.
lace for bib and bonnet.
ribbon for bonnet ties.
six large buttons.
scraps of felt for eyes and cheeks.
pink embroidery cotton.
scrap of wool for curls.

1. To make the head, transfer the patterns on page 74 and 75 onto tracing paper and cut out. Fold the fabric in half, right sides together. Pin the patterns to the fabric and cut out the pieces.

2. With right sides together, sew the back centre seam. Sew the head back to the head front round the outer edge, leaving the neck edge open. Turn through and stuff firmly to the edge of the neck.

3. Run a gathering thread round the neck edge, pull up the gathers tightly and sew the ends securely.

4. To make the hands, transfer the pattern on page 75 onto tracing paper and cut out. Pin the pattern to the fabric and cut out the pieces.

5. With right sides together, sew the hands in pairs, leaving the wrist edges open. Clip into the curves, turn through and stuff firmly.

6. Run a gathering thread round the wrist edges, pull up the gathers tightly and sew the ends securely.

7. To make the arms, trace the pattern on page 75 and cut out. Pin the pattern to the fabric and cut out the pieces.

8. Fold the arm fabric right sides together, and sew the underarm seams. Turn under a 2 cm (¾ in) hem along the wrist edges.

9. Position the hands in the wrist openings and sew round neatly. Stuff the arms but not too firmly, leaving the top 2 cm (¾ in) unstuffed.

10. To make the legs and feet, transfer the patterns on page 74 and 75 onto tracing paper and cut out. Pin the patterns to the fabric and cut out the pieces.

11. With right sides together, sew the legs in pairs round the outside edges, leaving the top and bottom edges open. Clip into the curves and turn through.

12. Pin the feet soles round the bottom edges of the legs and sew in position. Stuff the feet and ankles firmly, but stuff lightly towards the top of the legs, leaving the top 2 cm (¾ in) unstuffed.

13. To make the body, transfer the patterns on page 74 and 75 onto tracing paper and cut out. Pin the patterns to the fabric and cut out the pieces.

14. Run a gathering thread along the straight edge of the body bottom pieces and pull up the gathers slightly to fit across the body top pieces. Pin the bottoms to the tops and sew.

15. Tack the arms and legs in position on the body piece, with the raw edges parallel as shown in fig. 1.

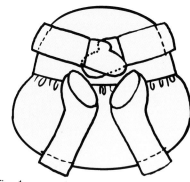

Fig. 1

16. Sew the body back to the body front, enclosing the arms and legs into the seams and leaving the neck edge open. (It makes it easier if you sew from one neck edge to between the legs, then repeat for the other side.) Turn through and stuff the body to give a soft, cuddly finish.

17. Turn under a small hem round the neck edge and run a gathering thread round the neck. Position the head in the neck opening up to the chin. Adjust the gathers evenly round the neck and sew securely all round.

18. To make the bib, transfer the pattern on page 74 onto tracing paper and cut out. Pin the pattern to the fabric and cut out the pieces.

19. With right sides together, sew lace round one bib piece.

20. With right sides together, sew the two bib pieces, leaving the neck edge open, and turn through.

21. Bind the neck edge with bias binding, leaving sufficient lengths at each side for the ties.

22. To make the bonnet, transfer the pattern on page 74 onto tracing paper and cut out. Pin the pattern to the fabric and cut out the bonnet.

23. Join A to B and sew a dart on each side of the bonnet. Turn under a 1 cm (⅜ in) hem at the neck edge and sew.

24. Run a gathering thread round the outer, curved edge and pull up the gathers to measure about 34 cm (13⅜ in). Mark the centre with a pin.

25. Cut a brim piece 38 cm x 8 cm (15 in x 3¼ in). Mark the centre of the long edge with a pin. Matching the centres, pin the right side of the brim to the wrong side (inside) of the bonnet's gathered edge and sew.

26. Fold the brim over to the front of the bonnet. Turn under a small hem on the brim edge and tack. Tuck in the excess of the brim at each side to make a neat edge, and topstitch in position.

27. Sew lace round the bonnet where it joins the brim.

28. Sew a length of ribbon to each side of the brim for ties. Sew a small curl of wool under the brim for hair.

29. *To make the nose,* follow the instructions on page 6, using a 6 cm (2⅜ in) diameter circle of the same fabric as for the head.

30. Embroider the mouth and sew on felt circles for the cheeks as shown in fig. 2. Glue on the eyes and add a sparkle with a tiny dot of white felt.

31. Sew buttons round the waistline – three at the front and three at the back.

Fig. 2 Full-size face

Fluffy Clowns

These cute clowns are very versatile and make wonderful mobiles, suspended from circles of cane. They can also be hung at different lengths in a bunch.
Their hair is made of marabou feathers, which can be bought by the metre and are available in pastel and primary colours from bridal shops and well-stocked haberdashers.
The clowns are 22 cm (8⅝ in) tall. They are not suitable as babies' toys, but they do make a lovely nursery wall decoration. Experiment with different facial expressions.

REQUIREMENTS

FOR EACH CLOWN

acrylic or poster paint.
3.5–4 cm (1⅜–1½ in) diameter wooden bead for the head, or use a pierced table tennis ball.
one pipe cleaner.
glue.
scraps of fabric.
polyester filling.
20 cm of 3 cm-wide (7⅞ in of 1¼ in-wide) lace.
25 cm (9⅞ in) narrow ribbon.
scrap of felt for hat.
cord for hanging.
tiny bell.
strong cotton.
about 13 cm (5 in) marabou feathers.
wool for pompons (optional).

1. To make the head, paint the wooden bead or table tennis ball as shown in fig. 1 or make your own expression and allow to dry.

Fig. 1

NOTE: *If you use poster paints, spray the finished face with a layer of varnish to protect the paint.*

2. Fold the pipe cleaner in half and push both ends through the bottom hole in the bead as shown in fig. 2. Drop glue into the top hole to secure the pipe cleaner. When dry, trim the ends.

glue

trim end of pipe cleaner

Fig. 2

3. To make the body, transfer the pattern on page 79 onto tracing paper and cut out. Pin the pattern to two pieces of fabric, right sides together.

4. Trace round the outline of the pattern and sew, leaving the neck edge open for turning through.

5. Cut out the body and clip into the corners, being careful not to clip too close to the stitches. Turn through.

6. Stuff the body firmly but not too stiffly. Sew the gap closed, leaving a small space in the middle for the pipe cleaner.

7. Push the loop of the pipe cleaner into this space and, using strong cotton, sew through the loop to each side of the neck, thus attaching the head to the body.

8. Stitch one end of the lace to the back of the neck. Run a gathering thread along the top edge of the lace, pull up the gathers to fit round the clown's neck and fold under the raw edge of the lace. Secure the lace to the back of the neck.

9. Using the ribbon, tie a bow round the clown's neck.

10. To make the hat, transfer the pattern on page 79 onto tracing paper and cut out. Pin the pattern to the felt and cut out the hat.

11. Overlap and glue the straight edges, forming a cone. Test whether the hat fits the head as you may have to adjust the size. Cut off the sharp point of the hat.

12. Tie a knot at one end of the cord and thread the cord through the hole so that the knot is inside the hat. Carefully drop a little glue onto the knot inside the hat to secure the cord.

13. Sew on the tiny bell, stuff the hat lightly and glue it onto the head.

14. Glue marabou feathers round the head, from ear to ear.

15. To make pompons, follow the instructions on page 7 and decorate the clown as shown in the photograph.

Acrobat Clowns

Each clown is 38 cm (15 in) tall. Make as many as you wish.
They can be joined using press studs.

REQUIREMENTS

FOR EACH CLOWN

two 42 cm x 15 cm (16½ in x 6 in)
  pieces contrasting fabric.
polyester filling.
two 8.5 cm (3⅜ in) diameter circles
  of non-stretch flesh-coloured fabric.
scraps of felt for face.
two 3 cm x 4 cm (1¼ in x 1½ in)
  pieces of felt for hair.
ribbon.
powder rouge.
glue.
black felt-tip pen.
two press studs.
22 cm of 1.5 cm (8⅝ in of ⅝ in)
  diameter dowel rod for swing.
22 cm x 8 cm (8⅝ in x 3¼ in) felt to
  cover dowel.
60 cm (23⅝ in) cord or ribbon for
  hanging.
two press studs for swing.

1. With right sides together, sew the two body pieces along the side seams (long edges), leaving a gap for turning through, as shown in fig. 1.

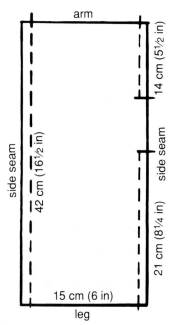

Fig. 1

2. Bring the side seams to the centre (the seam with the gap is the centre back seam). Match the centre seams and tack in position.

3. Make a mark on the centre back seam 13 cm (5⅛ in) from the arm edge and 16 cm (6¼ in) from the leg edge as shown in fig. 2.

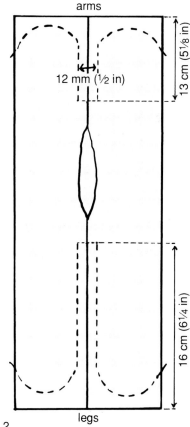

Fig. 2

4. Sew the arm and leg seams as shown in fig. 2, leaving 12 mm (½ in) between the two rows of stitching down the centre.

5. Remove the tacking stitches and cut between the two rows of stitching down the centre, to separate the arms and legs. Trim the rounded corners.

6. Clip into the curves and turn through.

7. Stuff the legs and arms to where they join the body, then topstitch a straight line across the tops of the legs and the bottoms of the arms as shown in fig. 3.

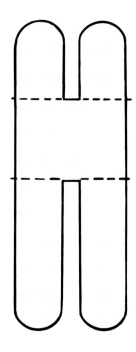

Fig. 3

8. Stuff the body and sew the gap closed.

9. *To make the head*, with right sides together, sew the two circles of flesh-coloured fabric round the outer edge, leaving a gap for turning through.

10. Turn through, stuff the head and sew the gap closed.

11. *To make the hat*, transfer the pattern on page 92 (coat hanger clown hat) onto tracing paper and cut out. Pin the pattern to the felt and cut out the hat.

12. Overlap and glue the straight edges to form a cone. Stuff the hat lightly and glue it onto the head, covering the sewn gap in the head seam.

13. *To make the hair*, cut slits into each piece of felt, as shown in fig. 4.

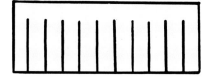

Fig. 4

14. Glue a strip of hair to each side of the face and round to the back of the head.

15. Glue black felt circles for the eyes, a red felt circle for the nose, and a v-shaped red felt mouth. Mark four lines round each eye with a black felt-tip pen, as shown in fig. 5, and rouge the cheeks.

Fig. 5   Full-size face

16. Glue the head to the body, applying glue to the centre back of the head, below the edge of the hat.

17. Tie a ribbon bow and glue or sew it to the chin.

18. *To make pompons*, follow the instructions on page 7, or cut felt circles of the size and quantity desired and glue onto the acrobat.

19. Sew on press studs – the pronged halves to the back of the hands and the flat halves to the front of the feet.

20. *To make the swing*, glue along one long edge of the felt and stick it to the dowel rod.

21. Roll the felt round the dowel and glue the other long edge in position.

22. Sew the flat halves of two press studs 8 cm (3¼ in) apart to the front of the swing, so that the acrobat clown can be attached to the swing.

23. Tie ribbon or cord to the sides of the swing and knot it at the top. Tie a loop in the centre of the ribbon for hanging.

Sweetie-pie Clown

This clown is 55 cm (21½ in) tall.
Using a small checked fabric for the head and hands creates an interesting contrast.
You can make this clown in primary colours too, in which case a yellow check for the face and hands works well, using red felt and embroidery cotton for the nose and mouth.

REQUIREMENTS
two 23 cm x 32 cm (9 in x 12⅝ in) pieces fine gingham fabric.
two 35 cm x 50 cm (13¾ in x 19¾ in) pieces fabric for body and hat.
two 35 cm x 50 cm (13¾ in x 19¾ in) pieces contrasting fabric for body and hat.
scraps of fabric for shoes.
polyester filling.
1 m x 7 cm-wide (1 yd 3 in x 2¾ in-wide) lace for neck frill.
two 41 cm x 3.5 cm-wide (16⅛ in x 1⅜ in-wide) pieces lace for ankle frills.
two 34 cm x 3.5 cm-wide (13⅜ in x 1⅜ in-wide) pieces lace for wrist frills.
wool for hair and pompons.
scraps of dark pink, black and white felt.
dark pink embroidery cotton.
black felt-tip pen.
1 m (1 yd 3 in) ribbon.
glue.
strong thread.

1. ***To make the clown,*** transfer the patterns on page 70 onto tracing paper and cut out. Pin the patterns to the fabric and cut out two head pieces, four hand pieces and four shoe pieces. Cut a hat piece, body piece and two arm pieces from each contrasting fabric.

2. With right sides together, sew the head back to the head front round the outer edge, leaving the neck edge open.

3. Clip into the curves and turn through. Stuff the head and neck firmly and sew the neck edges closed.

4. Sew two contrasting body pieces, right sides together, along the centre seam.

5. Repeat step 4, for the body front.

6. Sew a shoe piece to each ankle edge, matching Xs and Ys.

7. Sew a hand piece to each arm piece at the wrist edge.

8. With right sides together, sew the arms in pairs, matching the fabric and leaving each shoulder edge open.

9. Clip the curves and turn through.

10. Stuff the arms, leaving 1.5 cm (⅝ in) unstuffed at the shoulder edge, and sew the raw edges together close to the edge.

11. With right sides together, align the raw edges, match the dots as indicated on the pattern and tack the arms to the body front piece.

12. Matching the seam lines and leaving the neck edge open, pin and sew the body front to the body back round the outer edge, thus incorporating the arms into the seam.

13. Clip carefully into the corners and turn through.

14. Starting at the feet, stuff the body just enough to give a soft, even finish.

15. Starting at the centre back, turn under a small hem at the neck edge and run a gathering thread round the neck edge of the body piece. Insert the neck into the body, gently pushing the stuffing to the sides so that the neck fits. Pull up the gathers and sew the neck to the body.

16. ***To make the neck frill,*** stitch the top right corner of the right side of the lace to the centre back where the body joins the neck.

17. Run a gathering thread along the top edge of the lace to 1 cm (⅜ in) from the end and pull up the gathers to fit evenly round the neck. Turn under 1 cm (⅜ in) at the end of the lace and sew securely in position.

18. ***To make the wrist and ankle frills,*** make in the same way as the neck frill but stitch and gather down the centre of the lace. Begin and end at the underarm seam for the wrist frill. Begin and end at the inner leg seam for the ankle frill.

19. With right sides together, sew the hat pieces round the outer edge, leaving the straight edge open, and turn through.

20. Turn under and sew a 1 cm (⅜ in) hem at the straight edge. Stuff the hat lightly. Pin the hat in position on the head and sew.

21. ***To make the hair,*** follow the instructions on page 6. Wind the wool round three fingers for the back and sides of the head and round two fingers for the clown's fringe.

22. Sew the curls round the head on the join of the hat and the head.

23. Glue on the nose and eyes, with a white felt dot in each eye, and mark four lines round each eye with a waterproof black felt-tip pen as shown in fig. 1. Embroider the mouth.

Fig. 1 Full-size face

24. ***To make pompons,*** follow the instructions on page 7 and make 3 cm (1¼ in) diameter pompons. Sew or glue one to each shoe, three down the centre front of the body and one on the hat.

25. Using ribbon, tie a bow round the neck. Position the bow at the side and leave long ends.

Baby Clowns

These lovely clowns make soft, huggable toys. You can attach a bell to the top of the hat if the clown is not intended for a very young child.
For variation you can make a sweet Pierrot by using black and white fabric, and drawing a little tear below one eye.
The bodies are made in the same way as the bride doll on page 14.

REQUIREMENTS

FOR EACH CLOWN

body as for bride doll (see page 14).
two 58 cm x 40 cm (22⅞ in x 15¾ in) pieces contrasting fabric for clothes and hat.
112 cm x 9.5 cm (44 in x 3¾ in) fabric for neck frill.
polyester stuffing.
scraps of felt for eyes, nose and mouth.
powder rouge.
glue.
ribbon.
wool for hair.
two pompons.
black felt-tip pen.

1. *To make the body*, see steps 1-10 on page 14 and make the baby clown's body in the same way as the bride doll.

2. *To make the clothes*, transfer the pattern on page 65 onto tracing paper and cut out. Pin the pattern to the fabric and cut two pieces from each contrasting fabrics (double over the fabric to reverse the pattern).

3. With right sides together, join contrasting pieces of fabric and sew the centre seams to make the back and front.

4. With right sides together, sew the back to the front from the neck edges to the wrist edges.

5. Sew the underarm seams from the wrist edges to the ankle edges and then sew the inner leg seams. Turn through.

6. Turn under a double hem at the wrist and ankle edges, and sew neatly. Slip the clothes onto the body.

7. Run a gathering thread round the neck of the clothes and pull up the gathers to fit snugly round the neck. Sew in position, adjusting the gathers evenly, and secure the ends.

8. Run a gathering thread round the tunic's wrists and ankles, pull up the gathers tightly to form frills and secure the ends.

9. *To make the hat*, transfer the pattern on page 65 onto tracing paper and cut out. Pin the pattern to the fabric and cut two pieces from each contrasting fabric.

10. With right sides together, sew the hat pieces, alternating colours and leaving the bottom edge open.

11. Turn under the bottom edge of the hat and sew a small hem.

12. Stuff the hat lightly. Pin the hat onto the head and sew round firmly.

13. *To make the neck frill*, sew the short ends of the fabric right sides together to form a circle.

14. Turn under and sew a double hem along one long edge of the circle.

15. Turn under 1 cm (⅜ in) along the raw edge of the circle and run a gathering thread round.

16. Slip the neck frill over the head, pull up the gathers to fit snugly round the neck and sew the frill in position at the back of the neck.

Fig. 1 Full-size face

17. *To make the hair,* follow the instructions on page 6, making the curls approximately 3.5 cm (1⅜ in) long in front, but slightly longer at the sides and back of the head. Sew the curls to the head round the edge of the hat.

18. Using scraps of felt, glue on the eyes, nose and mouth or embroider the facial expressions. Mark four lines round each eye with a black felt-tip pen as shown in fig. 1. Follow the instructions on page 6 and rouge the cheeks.

19. Tie a ribbon bow round his neck.

20. *To make pompons,* follow the instructions on page 7. Sew one pompon to the hat and one to the centre front of the clothes.

Clown Coat Hanger

The pattern is designed for a child-size coat hanger measuring 31 cm (12¼ in) across.
You can either cut a full-size coat hanger down to this size or use the full-size hanger as is, adjusting the length of the arm tubes.

REQUIREMENTS
a wooden coat hanger.
a strip of wadding to pad the hanger.
strong thread.
two 18 cm x 13 cm (7 in x 5⅛ in) pieces fabric for arms.
two 8.5 cm (3⅜ in) diameter circles of flesh-coloured fabric for head.
two 16 cm (6¼ in) diameter circles of fabric for hands.
50 cm x 7 cm (19¾ in x 2¾ in) fabric for frill.
polyester filling.
tape or ribbon for wrist binding.
scrap of fake fur or wool.
scraps of felt.
tiny bell.
ribbon.
red embroidery cotton.
powder rouge.
glue.

1. Wind wadding round the coat hanger to pad it, covering the ends well. Secure by winding a length of strong thread round the wadding.

2. With right sides together, sew round the outer edge of the head circles, leaving a gap, and turn through. Stuff firmly and sew the gap closed.

3. Turn under a double hem of 6 mm (¼ in) along one short edge of each arm piece.

4. With right sides together, sew along the long edge of each strip, forming tubes.

5. Turn through and pull the arm tubes onto the coat hanger. Slide the tubes up to the centre of the coat hanger with the seams underneath.

6. Tuck in the raw edges at the centre and sew the two arm tubes together all the way round. Push up the hemmed edges to expose the padded ends of the hanger.

7. Run a gathering thread round the outer edge of each circle of fabric for the hands and slip a hand over each end of the hanger, covering the wadding. Pull up the gathers tightly and sew the ends down securely.

8. Sew the hemmed edges of the arm tubes to the hands. Glue or sew on a length of tape to cover the stitches, with the join of the tape at the bottom.

9. With right sides together, sew the two short edges of the frill. Turn under and sew a 6 mm (¼ in) double hem along one long edge.

10. Run a gathering thread round the raw edge of the frill, pull up the gathers tightly to form a circle and sew the ends securely. Sew the frill to the centre front of the coat hanger.

11. ***To make the hat,*** transfer the pattern on page 92 onto tracing paper and cut out. Pin the pattern to the felt and cut out the hat.

12. Overlap and glue the straight edges, forming a cone.

13. Stuff the hat lightly and glue it onto the clown's head, covering the join in the head seam.

14. Cut two small felt circles as shown in fig. 1 and glue to the hat for decoration.

Fig. 1 Full-size felt circle

15. Glue a small piece of fake fur, or sew a little curl from wool, to the edge of the hat at each side of the face.

16. Glue on the eyes and nose and embroider the mouth as shown in fig. 2. Rouge the cheeks and glue or sew the head to the centre of the frill.

Fig. 2 Full-size face

17. Thread a tiny bell onto a length of narrow ribbon and tie into a bow, incorporating the bell into the bow. Glue the bow to the chin.

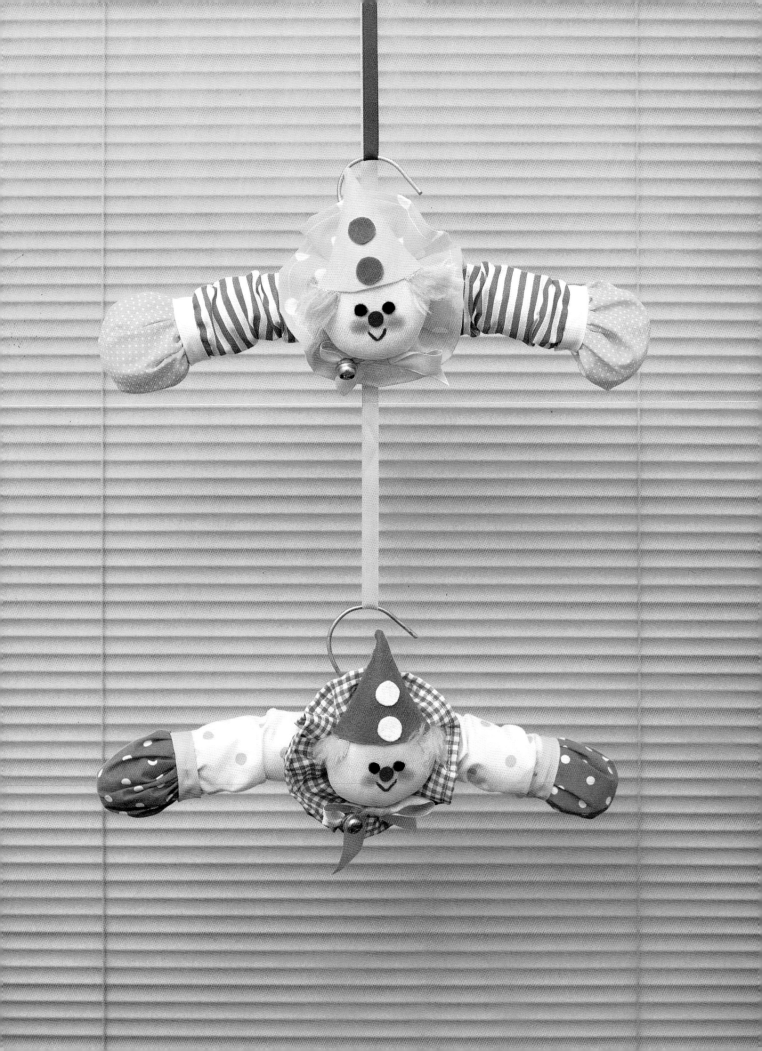

Pyjama Case Clown

The pyjama case clown measures 60 cm (24 in). Make it in colours to complement the bedroom. It looks lovely in pink or pastel colours too.

REQUIREMENTS

two 22 cm x 30 cm (8⅝ in x 11¾ in) pieces flesh-coloured fabric.
two 47 cm x 35 cm (18½ in x 13¾ in) pieces fabric for body and arms.
polyester stuffing.
28 cm x 20 cm (11 in x 7⅞ in) fabric for pocket.
34 cm x 34 cm (13⅜ in x 13⅜ in) fabric for shoes.
two 22 cm x 14 cm (8⅝ in x 5½ in) pieces fabric for hat.
two 24 cm x 24 cm (9½ in x 9½ in) pieces fabric for collar.
wool for hair and pompons.
scrap of red fabric for nose.
scraps of felt in black, red, white and pink for face.
five small bells.
1 m (1 yd 3 in) ribbon.
glue.
28 cm (11 in) of 6 mm-wide (¼ in-wide) elastic.

1. To make the head, transfer the pattern on page 73 onto tracing paper and cut out. Pin the pattern to the flesh-coloured fabric and cut out two head pieces on the fold.

2. With right sides together, sew the head pieces round the outer edge, leaving the neck edge open.

3. Clip into the corners at the neck and turn through. Stuff the head and neck firmly with polyester stuffing, making sure the head is well stuffed.

4. Using strong thread, run a gathering thread round the neck edge, pull up the gathers tightly and sew the ends securely.

5. To make the arms and hands, transfer the patterns on page 72 and 73 onto tracing paper and cut out. Pin the patterns to the flesh-coloured fabric and cut out four arm pieces and four head pieces. With right sides together, sew a hand piece to each arm piece at the wrist edge.

6. With right sides together, sew the arms in pairs, leaving the armhole edge open. Turn through and stuff the hand firmly, and the arm lightly to 2 cm (¾ in) from the top. Sew the raw edges closed. Repeat with the other arm.

7. To make the shoes, transfer the pattern on page 72 onto tracing paper and cut out. Pin the pattern to the fabric and cut out the pieces.

8. With right sides together, sew the shoes in pairs round the outer edge, leaving the ankle edge open.

9. Clip into the curves, turn through and stuff to 2 cm (¾ in) from each edge. Bring the seams to the centre and sew closed across the top of each shoe.

10. To make the pocket, transfer the pattern on page 73 onto tracing paper and cut out. Pin the pattern to the fabric and cut out the pocket piece. Turn under and sew a 6 mm (¼ in) double hem along the top edge of the fabric.

11. Measure a 28 cm (11 in) length of elastic and, on the wrong side of the pocket, pin the elastic on the hemline, leaving 1.5 cm (⅝ in) of elastic over each side of the pocket. (The short lengths of elastic at each side will give a hold at the beginning and end of stitching.)

12. Stretch the elastic out to the length of the pocket and stitch it in position, using a zig-zag stitch.

13. To make the body, transfer the pattern on page 72 onto tracing paper and cut out. Pin the pattern to the fabric and cut out the body pieces.

14. Position the pocket, wrong side down, to the right side of one body piece and pin, starting at the centre bottom.

15. Using a 1 cm (⅜ in) seam allowance, sew the pocket to the body.

16. Pin the arms and legs to the right side of the body front and sew in position as shown in fig. 1.

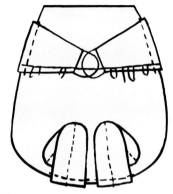

Fig. 1

17. With right sides together, sew the body back to the body front round the outer edge. Use a 1 cm (⅜ in) seam allowance, thus incorporating the arms and legs into the seam, leaving the neck edge open. Turn through.

18. Turn under a 1 cm (⅜ in) hem at the neck edge of the body.

19. Run a gathering thread round the neck edge, starting at the centre back. Slip the head inside the neck edge of the body, right up to the chin and pull up the gathers tightly. Adjust the gathers evenly round, matching the side seams of the body to the side seams of the head. Sew the body all round the neck securely.

20. To make the hat, transfer the pattern on page 72 onto tracing paper and cut out. Pin the traced pattern to the fabric and cut out the pieces.

21. With right sides together, sew the hat pieces round the outer edge, leaving the straight edge open. Turn through.

22. Turn under and sew a 1 cm (⅜ in) hem round the bottom edge of the hat.

23. Stuff the top of the hat, position it on the head with pins and sew on securely.

24. To make the collar, transfer the pattern on page 73 onto tracing paper and cut out. Pin the pattern to the fabric and cut out the collar pieces.

25. With right sides together, sew the two collar pieces all the way round (including neck edge), leaving a gap for turning through.

26. Clip into the corners and round the neck edge. Trim the seams close to the stitching at the points.

27. Turn through, pushing out the points with the blunt end of a crochet hook and sew the gap closed.

28. Position the collar round the neck, covering the join of the head and body. Secure each end of the collar at the centre back of the neck and sew a little bell onto each point (Do not sew bells onto the centre back half-points.)

29. *To make the nose,* follow the instructions on page 6 and use a 5 cm (2 in) diameter circle of red fabric. Sew the nose to the face.

30. *To make the hair,* follow the instructions on page 6. Wind the wool round three fingers for the back and sides and round two fingers for the fringe.

31. Glue on the eyes and decorate the face as shown in fig. 2. Glue or sew a piece of ribbon round the wrists, starting at the underarm seams. Turn under the ribbon ends to neaten.

32. Tie a length of ribbon into a bow round the clown's neck.

33. *To make the pompons,* follow the instructions given on page 7 and make three 4.5 cm (1¾ in) diameter pompons. Glue or sew a pompon to the hat and one to each shoe.

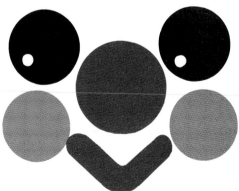

Fig. 2   Full-size face

NOTE: *Use a 1 cm (⅜ in) seam allowance unless otherwise indicated.*

Jingles The Clown

Jingles is wonderful for sitting around. His legs and arms have sewn 'joints', making all kinds of positions possible. He is 94 cm (37 in) tall.

REQUIREMENTS
80 cm x 31 cm (31½ in x 12¼ in) flesh-coloured fabric for head and arms (not stretch fabric).
42 cm x 27 cm (16½ in x 10⅝ in) fabric for body.
two 45 cm x 19 cm (17¾ in x 7½ in) pieces striped fabric for legs.
40 cm x 28 cm (15¾ in x 11 in) fabric for shoes.
48 cm x 26 cm (18⅞ in x 10¼ in) fabric for hat.
48 cm x 26 cm (18⅞ in x 10¼ in) contrasting fabric for hat.
two 62 cm x 32 cm (24½ in x 12⅝ in) pieces fabric for shirt.
7 cm (2¾ in) diameter circle of red fabric for nose.
58 cm (22⅞ in) of bias binding for neck of shirt.
polyester filling.
wool for pompons and hair.
ribbon for neck.
braid or ric-rac for trimming.
black felt-tip pen.
two bells.
scraps of blue, black, red and white felt.
one press stud.
powder rouge.
glue.

1. *To make the shoes and legs,* transfer the pattern on page 69 onto tracing paper and cut out. Pin the pattern to the fabric and cut out four shoe pieces.

2. With right sides together, sew the shoe pieces in pairs, down the centre front seam, starting at the ankle edge and sewing 3 cm (1¼ in) as shown in fig. 1.

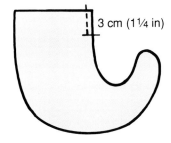

3 cm (1¼ in)

Fig. 1

3. Open out the shoes and, with right sides together, pin a shoe to the end of each leg piece. Sew in position as shown in fig. 2.

Fig. 2

4. With right sides together, fold each leg in half and, starting at the top of the leg, sew each leg seam and the rest of the shoe seam as shown in fig. 3. Clip into the curves and turn through.

Fig. 3

5. Measure and mark a point 20 cm (7⅞ in) up from each ankle edge. Stuff the shoe and legs firmly up to about 2 cm (¾ in) from the marked level.

6. With the leg seam to the centre back, stitch across the leg, at the marked level, to make the knee joint.

7. Continue stuffing the legs up to 2 cm (¾ in) from the raw edge. Sew the raw edge closed.

8. *To make the arms,* transfer the pattern on page 69 onto tracing paper and cut out. Pin the traced pattern to the fabric and cut out two arms on the fold.

9. With right sides together, sew the underarm seams as shown in fig. 4, leaving the top raw edges open. Clip into the curves and turn through.

Fig. 4

10. Mark a point 18 cm (7 in) up from each hand edge. Stuff up to 2 cm (¾ in) from this mark and sew across the arms to make the elbow joints.

11. Continue stuffing the arms to 2 cm (¾ in) from the raw edge. Sew the raw edge closed.

12. *To make the head and body,* transfer the patterns on page 68 and 69 onto tracing paper and cut out. Pin the patterns to the fabric and cut out two head pieces and two body pieces.

13. With right sides together, sew a head piece to the top edge of each body piece, in the centre of the shoulders. Pin and tack the arms and legs into position on the right side of one body piece as shown in fig. 5.

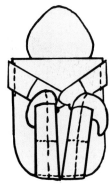

Fig. 5

19. Turn under and sew a 6 mm (¼ in) double hem at each wrist edge of the shirt. Sew braid or trimming along the hemmed edges. Sew the underarm seams and clip into the corners. Turn through.

20. Turn under and sew a 6 mm (¼ in) double hem along the bottom edge of the shirt. Sew braid or trimming along the hemmed edge.

21. Sew a press stud to the bias binding at the centre back to close the shirt.

22. *To make the hat,* transfer the pattern on page 69 onto tracing paper and cut out. Pin the traced pattern to the fabric and cut out two hat pieces from shoe fabric and two from shirt fabric.

23. Take one piece of each fabric and cut along the dotted line as shown on the pattern, to form the hat fronts.

24. With right sides together, sew down the centre seam of the hat back pieces and the hat front pieces.

25. Sew the hat back to the hat front round the outer edge, leaving the neck and face edge open. Clip into the curves and turn through.

26. Turn under a 1 cm (⅜ in) hem at the neck edge, a 6 mm (¼ in) hem at the face edge, and sew. Stuff the points of the hat firmly with polyester filling.

27. Pin the hat to the head, tucking in stuffing where necessary, and sew neatly all the way round. Sew a bell to the point of each hat.

28. *To make the hair,* follow the instructions on page 6, wrap wool round three of your fingers to make a curl and sew it to the centre front of the forehead.

29. *To make a nose,* follow the instructions on page 6 and sew in position.

30. Glue on the eyes and mouth and rouge the cheeks. Mark four lines round the eyes with the black felt-tip pen as shown in fig. 6.

31. Using ribbon, tie a bow round neck.

32. *To make pompons,* follow the instructions on page 7. Make five pompons, sew three down the shirt front and one onto each shoe.

14. With right sides together, sew the body back to the body front, thus enclosing the raw edges of the arms and legs into the seam. This will be a bit difficult, with not much room to accommodate the legs and arms inside the body. Sew the body in short sections, stopping to move the limbs out of the way for the next section, making sewing easier. Leave a large gap in the seam at the top of the head for turning through.

15. Clip carefully into the curves and turn through.

16. Stuff the body and head firmly. Sew the gap in the head seam closed, adding more stuffing as you sew.

17. *To make the shirt,* transfer the pattern on page 68 onto tracing paper and cut out. Pin the pattern to the fabric and cut out the pieces.

18. With right sides together, sew the shoulder seams. Cut an 11 cm (4⅜ in) slit down the centre back from the neck edge. Bind the neck and back slit edge with bias binding.

Fig. 6   Full-size face

Busy Bear

As well as making a lovely wall-hanging this bear, which is 95 cm (37½ in) tall, also teaches children to master a zip, press stud, hook and eye, button, buckle and to tie shoe laces. Sew all of these on securely.

REQUIREMENTS

50 cm (19¾ in) fake fur for head and paws.
a pair of safety eyes and a safety nose.
polyester filling.
two 52 cm x 30 cm (20½ in x 11¾ in) pieces fabric for shoulder support.
two 52 cm x 22 cm (20½ in x 8⅝ in) pieces fabric for shirt.
two 46 cm x 36 cm (18⅛ in x 14¼ in) pieces fabric for trousers.
14 cm x 25 cm (5½ in x 9⅞ in) fabric for zip pocket.
14.5 cm x 13 cm (5¾ in x 5⅛ in) fabric for button pocket.
22 cm x 36 cm (8⅝ in x 14¼ in) fabric for bow tie.
54 cm x 36 cm (21¼ in x 14¼ in) fabric for shoes.
16 cm x 15 cm (6¼ in x 6 in) fabric for press stud tab.
22 cm x 16 cm (8⅝ in x 6¼ in) fabric for hook and eye tab.
50 cm (19¾ in) belting.
buckle to fit belting.
strong thread.
three large buttons.
scrap of felt for buttonhole strap.
large hook and eye.
large press stud.
47 cm of 8 mm (18½ in of ⅜ in) diameter dowel rod.
15 cm (6 in) zip.
one pair bootlaces.
ribbon.

1. *To make the head,* transfer the patterns on page 89 and 90 onto tracing paper and cut out. Pin the patterns to the fabric and cut out the pieces.

2. With right sides together, sew the ears in pairs, leaving the bottom edge open, and turn through.

3. Tack the ears to the side front pieces round the top of the side front pieces from A to B, as indicated on the pattern.

4. With right sides together, sew the centre front piece to the side front pieces, matching Xs and Ys.

5. Sew the nose piece to the sewn front head piece, matching Cs and Ds. Sew the centre seam of the nose and continue sewing the seam, thus joining the two side front pieces below the nose.

6. With right sides together, sew the two darts on the head back piece.

7. Sew the dart in each side front piece as indicated on the pattern.

8. Pierce the fabric at the eye and nose positions and push the prongs of the safety eyes and nose through to the back. Push the safety discs onto the prongs, cup-shape outwards as shown in fig. 1.

Fig. 1

9. With right sides together, sew the head back to the head front. Turn through and stuff the head firmly.

10. *To make the paws and shoulder supports,* transfer the patterns on page 88 onto tracing paper. Pin the pattern to the fur and cut out four paw pieces. Sew the paws in pairs, right sides together, leaving the straight edge open. Turn through and stuff with polyester stuffing.

11. Trim 5 cm (2 in) off the bottom edge of one shoulder support piece.

12. Turn under and sew a 1 cm (⅜ in) hem at the side edge of each shoulder support piece.

13. Right side out, fold the wider shoulder support piece in half length-wise and sew 2 cm (¾ in) from folded edge as shown in fig. 2, forming a casing for the dowel rod.

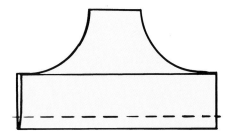

Fig. 2

14. With right sides together, sew the two shoulder support pieces along the curved edges and along the bottom edge.

15. Turn through the neck and sew the side openings closed, leaving the casing free. Stuff the shoulder support firmly.

16. Run a gathering thread round the neck edge, pull up the gathers tightly and secure the ends.

17. Push the bear's head well over the neck of the shoulder support, with the casing at the back, and sew the head securely to the neck.

18. Slide the dowel rod into the casing and sew the sides of the casing closed.

19. Pull the paws over the ends of the shoulder support and sew in position.

20. *To make the trousers,* cut the fabric as shown in fig. 3 and trace and cut out the pattern for the shoe (page 90). Pin the shoe pattern to the fabric and cut out four shoe pieces. Sew a shoe piece to each trouser bottom edge with the toes pointing outwards.

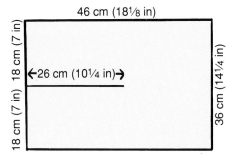

Fig. 3

21. Cut bootlaces into four 61 cm (24 in) lengths and sew to the shoe pieces as shown in fig. 4, using a zig-zag stitch and sewing to approximately 4 cm (1½ in) from the centre front edge of each shoe.

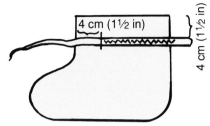

Fig. 4

22. *To make the shirt,* transfer the pattern on page 88 onto tracing paper and cut out. Pin the pattern to the fabric and cut out the shirt back and front. With right sides together, sew the shirt back and front to the trouser back and front.

23. *To make the zip pocket,* cut the piece of fabric in half lengthwise.

24. With right sides together, sew the two pocket pieces along one long edge (centre seam), leaving a space in the middle to fit the zip.

25. Sew the zip into the space, turn under a small hem all round the edge of the zip pocket and tack.

26. Position the zip pocket as shown in fig. 5 and sew it to the trouser front.

27. *To make the hook and eye tab,* transfer the pattern on page 89 onto tracing paper and cut out. Pin the traced pattern to the fabric and cut out the pieces.

28. With right sides together, sew round the outer edge of the hook and eye pieces, leaving the short straight edge open.

29. Turn through and tuck the raw edges to the inside of the tab. Topstitch round the edge. Position the tab as shown in fig. 5 and sew along the short edge to the trouser front.

30. Sew a hook and eye to the point of the tab – the hook on the tab and the eye on the trouser front.

31. *To make the button pocket,* turn under and sew a 6 mm (¼ in) double hem along one 13 cm (5⅛ in) edge. Turn under and tack the other three edges of the pocket.

32. *To make the buttonhole tab,* transfer the pattern on page 88 onto tracing paper and cut out. Pin the pattern to the felt and cut out the pieces.

33. Sew round the outer edge, using a close zig-zag stitch and leaving the straight edges open.

34. Mark the length of the buttonhole required, zig-zag round this mark and carefully slit down the middle of the buttonhole stitching.

35. Sew the button pocket to the trouser front as shown in fig. 5, sewing the raw edges of the buttonhole strap into the seam as shown in fig. 6.

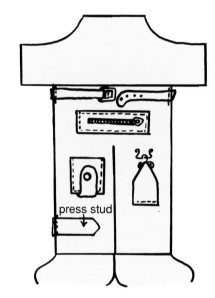

Fig. 5

Fig. 6

36. Fold the strap up on to the pocket and sew the button in position on the pocket.

37. *To make the press stud tab,* transfer the pattern on page 89 onto tracing paper and cut out. Pin the pattern to the fabric and cut out the pieces.

38. With right sides together, sew round the outer edge, leaving the straight short edge open. Turn through and topstitch round the sewn edge.

39. Tack the press stud tab in position on the trouser front as shown in fig. 5, aligning the raw edge with the side of the trouser leg. Sew one half of the press stud on the point of the tab, and the other half to the trouser front.

40. *To make the belt,* cut the belting in half widthwise and thread the buckle onto one piece.

41. Sew the buckle onto the end of the belting securely. Pierce holes at one end of the other piece and do up the buckle.

42. Lay the belt across the front body piece at the waistline, with the buckle at the centre. Sew the belt to each side of the trouser front. Cut away excess belting at each side.

43. Sew the body back to the body front: sew one shoulder seam, leaving the wrist edge open, and continue sewing from the lower wrist edge right round the body and shoes, up to the other lower wrist edge as shown in fig. 7.

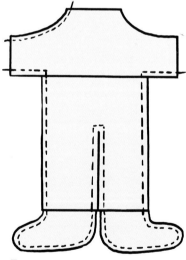

Fig. 7

44. Clip into the curves and turn through.

45. Sew two buttons on the shirt front. Turn under 1 cm (⅜ in) at the neck edge and sew.

46. Sew a 1 cm (⅜ in) hem on each open shoulder edge.

47. Stuff the shoes firmly.

48. Slip the body onto the shoulder support and pin, joining the two open shoulder edges, and sew in place. Sew the open shoulder seam closed.

49. Turn under a 1 cm (⅜ in) hem at the wrist edges of the sleeves and sew the sleeves to the paws.

50. With right sides together, sew the long edges of the bow tie piece and turn through.

51. Centre the seam and fold the short raw edges at each side to the back to meet in the centre. Sew the raw edges together as shown in fig. 8.

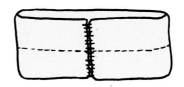

Fig. 8

52. Tie a piece of ribbon round the middle and knot it at the back.

53. Slip a length of ribbon through the back of the loop round the centre of the bow tie. Tie the ribbon round the bear's neck with the knot at the back and the bow tie at the centre front.

54. Sew a loop of tape securely to the back of the head for hanging the bear.

Happy Faces

These fun wall decorations really brighten up a room, and are simple to make. Use a colour combination to match the décor of the room. A black and white Happy Face is also very striking. A glue gun is an extremely useful tool to use when making these decorations, as there is quite a lot of glueing to do.

REQUIREMENTS

25.5 cm (10 in) diameter firm cardboard circle or thin silver cake board.

33 cm (13 in) diameter circle of fabric (to match frills).

22 cm (8⅝ in) diameter thin card for covering the back.

two 19 cm (7½ in) diameter circles of flesh-coloured fabric.

2 m x 12 cm (2¼ yd x 4¾ in) fabric for outer frill.

2 m x 8 cm (2¼ yd x 3¼ in) fabric for inner frill.

tape or cord for hanging.

polyester filling.

glue.

ribbon for bow.

scrap of fabric for nose.

black felt-tip pen.

powder rouge.

scraps of felt for eyes, mouth and hat.

wool for hair and pompons.

1. To make the backing, cut a small hole 1 cm (⅜ in) from the edge of the firm cardboard circle. Thread about 16 cm (6¼ in) of tape through the hole and tie the ends to form a loop.

2. Cover one side of the cardboard circle with the fabric circle (right side out). Take excess fabric over the edge of the cardboard to the other side, overlapping and glueing it in position. You will have to make a slit in the fabric when you come to the loop.

3. Glue the thin card circle over the untidy side of the covered circle.

4. To make the face, with right sides together, sew the two flesh-coloured circles round the outer edge, leaving a gap for turning through. Turn through and stuff. Sew the gap closed.

5. To make the hat, transfer the pattern on page 67 onto tracing paper and cut out. Pin the traced pattern to the felt and cut out the hat.

6. Overlap and glue the straight edges, forming a cone. Stuff the hat lightly. Glue or sew the hat onto the head, covering the sewn gap.

7. To make a pompon, follow the instructions given on page 7 and decorate the hat.

8. To make the hair, follow the instructions on page 6. Sew three thick curls, each 6 cm (2⅜ in) long, to each side of the face, down the seam.

9. To make the nose, follow the instructions on page 6.

10. Sew or glue the eyes, nose and mouth in position and mark four lines round each eye with a felt-tip pen as shown in fig. 1. Rouge the cheeks.

11. To make the frills, turn under a double hem along three edges of each frill piece, leaving one long edge free.

12. Mark the centre of each frill piece to help you to adjust the gathers evenly, then run a gathering thread along the unhemmed edge of each frill.

13. Pull up the gathers of the outer frill and, starting at the bottom edge directly opposite the hanging loop, glue the frill round the cardboard circle about 2.5 cm (1 in) from the edge. The centre mark should fall at the point where the hanging loop is.

14. Pull up the gathers of the inner frill and glue it about 2 cm (¾ in) in from outer frill.

15. Glue the head to the centre of the frills and position it so that it hangs straight.

16. Using a ribbon, tie a bow and sew or glue it under the chin.

Fig. 1 Full-size face

Doorstops

These attractive doorstops are an appealing and practical solution to the problem of banging doors.
The three designs given are made similarly, although the measurements vary slightly.
To make the weight for the doorstops, put bags of fish tank gravel, pebbles or a rock inside each body.

GRANNY SHEEP
approximately 35 cm (13¾ in) tall

REQUIREMENTS
glue.
strong cotton.
polyester filling.
weight for inside body.
red embroidery cotton for mouth.
20 cm (7⅞ in) diameter firm cardboard circle.
33 cm x 66 cm (13 in x 26 in) fabric strip for body.
two 20 cm x 25 cm (7⅞ in x 9⅞ in) pieces fabric for arms.
28 cm (11 in) diameter circle of same fabric to cover the base.
56 cm x 23 cm (22 in x 9 in) fleecy fabric for head and ears.
scraps of lace and ribbon.
a crocheted shawl or a triangle of soft fabric.
wire and gold cord for spectacles.
wooden meat skewers for knitting needles.
wooden beads to fit ends of skewers.
scrap of wool for knitting.
two 20 cm (7⅞ in) squares of black felt for the nose, ears, eyes and hands.

1. *To make the head,* transfer the patterns on page 85 onto tracing paper and cut out. Pin the patterns to the fabric and cut out the head, ear and nose pieces.

2. With right sides together, sew contrasting pieces of the ears, leaving the bottom edges open and turn through. Sew a little pleat at the bottom edges of the ears.

3. With right sides together, sew the nose pieces to the front head pieces.

4. With right sides together, sew the head back centre seam and tack the ear edges to the head fronts.

5. With right sides together, sew the two head front pieces along the front edge down to the neck.

6. With right sides together, sew the head back to the head front, sewing the ears into the seam and leaving the neck edge open. Turn through and stuff the sheep's head firmly.

7. Run a gathering thread round the neck, pull up the gathers slightly and secure the ends.

8. Glue on the eyes as shown in fig. 1 and embroider the mouth, using long stitches round the snout.

Fig. 1

9. *To make the body,* run a gathering thread round the edge of the fabric circle. Place the cardboard circle in the centre of the fabric circle, pull up the gathers evenly and sew the ends securely.

10. With right sides together, sew the two short ends of the fabric strip for the body, forming a tube, and turn through.

11. Turn under a 1.5 cm (⅝ in) hem along one raw edge and sew.

12. With the covered side of the cardboard to the outside, sew the body tube to the covered cardboard base.

13. Stuff the body a quarter of the way up with polyester stuffing, then put the weight inside. Continue stuffing the body up to the neck edge.

14. Run a gathering thread round the neck, pull up the gathers tightly and sew the ends securely.

15. Sew the head to the body, matching the back seams. Run a gathering thread round the body, 14.5 cm (5¾ in) up from the base. Pull up the gathers to make the waist and sew the ends securely.

16. Sew or glue a ruffle of lace round the base of the body and the neck.

17. Sew or glue ribbon round the base of the body and the waist.

18. Using ribbon, tie bows and glue to the centre front waistline and to each ear.

19. *To make the hands,* transfer the pattern on page 85 onto tracing paper and cut out. Pin the pattern to the black felt, and cut out four hand pieces.

20. With right sides together, sew the hands in pairs, leaving the wrist edges open. Turn through, stuff firmly and sew closed.

21. *To make the arms*, fold each arm piece lengthwise with right sides together, and sew the underarm seam (long edges). Bring the underarm seam to the centre and run a gathering thread through both thicknesses along one short edge. Pull up the gathers tightly and secure the ends to complete the shoulder end. Turn through.

22. Turn under a 2 cm (¾ in) hem at each wrist edge and pin. Stuff the arms lightly.

23. Run a gathering thread round each arm, 1 cm (⅜ in) from the wrist edge. Insert the hands, pull up the gathers to fit snugly round the hands and sew in position. Glue ribbon round to cover the gathering stitches.

24. Sew the arms to the body at the shoulder position.

25. *To make a pair of spectacles*, push wire through the centre of a gold tube-type cord. Form the wire into a circle with a diameter of approximately 3.5 cm (1⅜ in). Bend the rest of the cord into the curve for the bridge of the nose and another circle for the other half of the spectacles. Glue or sew the ends of the wire/cord securely. Sew the pair of spectacles onto the nose.

26. To make the knitting, knit up a small square of garter stitch (plain).

27. Cut two wooden skewers to measure 15 cm (6 in). Push wooden beads onto the ends and glue. Sharpen the cut end of each skewer with a penknife. Slip the knitting onto the skewers and secure the stitches with glue.

28. Roll the wool from the knitting into a little ball.

29. Sew the arms of the sheep onto the skirt in a 'knitting' position. Sew the ske- wers onto the inside of the hands and glue the ball of wool to the hem of the sheep's skirt.

30. To make a shawl, use a triangular piece of soft fabric, or crochet the shawl using double knitting wool and a size 4.50 crochet hook.

31. Chain 7, treble 1 into the 6th chain from the hook, chain 5 and turn. 2nd row: treble 2 into the top of the first treble, treble 3 into the space between the next treble and the turning chain then, chain 5 and turn.

32. Repeat, starting each row with treble 2 into the first treble (of previous row), treble 1 into each of the next trebles and ending with treble 3 into the space be- tween the last treble and the turning chain, chain 5.

33. When the shawl is large enough round the shoulders and the ends meet at the centre front, end off. Sew in the ends of the yarn and attach the shawl to the sheep's body with a press stud or a loop and button.

MOTHER ELEPHANT AND TWINS
approximately 48 cm (19 in) tall

REQUIREMENTS
glue.
strong cotton.
polyester filling.
weight for inside body.
red embroidery cotton for mouth.
20 cm (7⅞ in) diameter firm cardboard circle.
38 cm x 66 cm (15 in x 26 in) fabric
  strip for body.
two 20 cm x 28 cm (7⅞ in x 11 in)
  pieces fabric for arms.
28 cm (11 in) diameter circle of
  same fabric to cover the base.
50 cm (19¾ in) fake fur for head,
  ears and babies.
130 cm x 6.5 cm (51⅛ in x 2⅝ in)
  strip for frill.
35 cm x 8.5 cm (13¾ in x 3⅜ in)
  strip for bonnet.
29 cm x 4.5 cm (11½ in x 1¾ in)
  strip for bonnet binding.
scraps of felt.
scraps of lace and ribbon.
scraps of brushed nylon for baby
  blankets.
two press studs.

1. ***To make the mother elephant's head,*** transfer the patterns on page 86 and 87 onto tracing paper and cut out. Pin the patterns to the fur fabric (checking the direction of the stroke of the fur) and cut out two front head pieces, one back head piece and four ears.

2. With right sides together, sew the ears in pairs, leaving the straight edge open, and turn through.

3. With right sides together, sew the head fronts round the outer edge, leaving the neck edge and sides open, and turn through.

4. Tack the ear edges to the head fronts. Sew the head back to the head front, enclosing the ears into the seam, leaving the neck edge open.

5. Turn the head through to the right side and stuff firmly, pushing the stuffing well into the trunk.

6. Run a gathering thread round the neck, pull up the gathers and sew the ends down securely.

7. Using felt, cut out a pair of eyes as shown in fig. 2. Using black felt, cut out two strips 3 cm x 1.5 cm (1¼ in x ⅝ in) for the eyelashes.

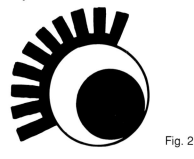
Fig. 2

8. Cut slits into the eyelash strip. Fan out the eyelashes and glue them round the eyes. Embroider the mouth.

9. ***To make the body,*** follow steps 9-15 as for the granny sheep, but use the measurements given for the elephant. Make the waistline 20 cm (7⅞ in) up from the base of the body.

10. With right sides together, sew the short ends of the frill fabric, forming a circle. Turn under a double hem along one long edge, tack and then sew on some lace along this edge.

11. Run a gathering stitch along the raw edge and slip the frill round the base. Adjust the gathers and sew the frill in position round the body.

12. Sew or glue lace and ribbon round the base to cover the gathering stitches.

13. ***To make the arms and hands,*** follow steps 19-24 as for the granny sheep, but use the measurements given for the elephant. Cut the hand pieces (pattern on page 86) from the same fur fabric as for the head.

14. ***To make the bonnet,*** turn under and sew a double hem on three sides of the strip, leaving one long edge free.

15. Run a gathering thread along the free edge and pull up the gathers to measure 26 cm (10¼ in).

16. Using the strip of bonnet binding, bind the gathered edge of the bonnet, tucking in 1.5 cm (⅝ in) at each end. Sew a length of ribbon to each side of the bonnet and tie it under the chin.

17. Sew a press stud to each hand and on both sides of the skirt at the front, so that the hands and arms are in the correct position to hold the twins.

18. To make the elephant twins, refer to the patterns on page 67 and follow steps 7–15 on page 10 as shown in Novelty bibs but use fake fur and stuff the whole body. Omit the arms and don't gather round the neck.

19. Cut a small square of brushed nylon to wrap each elephant baby in and sew it on.

SOLDIER
approximately 52 cm (20½ in) tall

REQUIREMENTS
glue.
strong cotton.
polyester filling.
weight for inside body.
red embroidery cotton for mouth.
18 cm (7 in) diameter firm cardboard circle.
60 cm x 22 cm (23⅝ in x 8⅝ in)
   red fabric for body top.
two 20 cm x 28 cm (7⅞ in x 11 in)
   pieces red fabric for arms.
60 cm x 20 cm (23⅝ in x 7⅞ in)
   black fabric for body bottom.
26 cm (10¼ in) diameter circle of
   black fabric.
24 cm x 22 cm (9½ in x 8⅝ in) flesh-
   coloured cotton knit fabric for
   head and hands.
48 cm x 24 cm (19 in x 9½ in) fake
   fur for hat and moustache.
powder rouge.
white tape for belt
black tape for collar, cuffs and
   chin-strap.
one small gold buckle.
gold braid.
six large buttons and two small
   gold buttons.
scraps of felt.
one press stud.

1. To make the head and hands, transfer the patterns on page 84 onto tracing paper and cut out. Pin the patterns to the fabric and cut out the pieces.

2. With right sides together, sew the head centre back seam and then sew the head back to the head front, leaving the neck edge open.

3. With right sides together, sew the hands in pairs, leaving the wrist edges open for turning through.

4. Turn through and stuff the head and hands firmly.

5. Run a gathering thread round the neck, pull up the gathers and sew the ends down securely.

6. To make the nose, follow the instructions on page 6, using a 6 cm (2⅜ in) diameter circle cut from the flesh-coloured fabric.

7. Sew the nose onto the face, rouge the cheeks and glue on the eyes as shown in fig. 3. Embroider the mouth and a dimple in the chin. Glue on a strip of fake fur for the moustache.

Fig. 3

8. To make the body and arms, sew the red body top fabric to the black body bottom fabric along the long edge, using a 1 cm (⅜ in) seam.

9. Follow steps 9-15 as for the granny sheep, but use the measurements given for the soldier. Make the waistline 3.5 cm (1⅜ in) up from the join of the red and black body pieces.

10. Thread the buckle onto white tape and glue it round the waist, positioning the buckle at the centre front.

11. Glue a strip of black tape and gold braid round the wrist edges. Sew buttons on the cuffs, positioning them at the outer sides of the arms.

12. To make the hat, transfer the patterns on page 84 onto tracing paper and cut out. Pin the patterns to fake fur or felt and cut one back and one front piece.

13. With right sides together, sew round the outer edges of the hat, leaving the face edge open. Turn through and stuff the top of the hat firmly.

14. Put the hat on the head, pushing the head in well. Sew the hat to the head, making a little pleat at the back of the hat, and glue a strip of black tape to each side of the head for a chin strap.

15. Glue a strip of black tape round the neck for a collar and a strip of gold braid below the collar.

16. Sew gold buttons down the front and sew a press stud onto one hand and the hat so that the soldier can salute.

Calico Cat

This cat is 38 cm (15 in) tall and can easily be made into a door-stop by putting a weight into the body.

REQUIREMENTS
50 cm (19¾ in) calico for body, tail and gusset.
two 80 cm x 20 cm (31½ in x 7⅞ in) pieces floral fabric for legs.
4 m of 3.5 cm-wide (4 yd 1 ft of 1⅜ in-wide) lace.
polyester filling.
black felt-tip pen.
strong thread.
88 cm x 12 cm (34⅝ in x 4¾ in) fabric for bow.

1. To make the body, transfer the patterns on page 82 and 83 onto tracing paper and cut out. Pin the patterns to the fabric and cut out two body pieces, four front leg and four back leg pieces, and two tail pieces. Cut out a 50 cm x 9 cm (19¾ in x 3½ in) strip of calico for the gusset and trim the ends as shown.

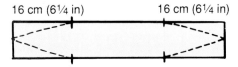

16 cm (6¼ in)   16 cm (6¼ in)

Fig. 1

2. On the right side of one body piece, draw the face using a black felt-tip pen.

3. With right sides together, sew the gusset to one body piece, between the points, as indicated on the pattern.

4. With right sides together, sew the body pieces, starting at the centre of the gusset and leaving a 12 cm (4¾ in) gap in the gusset seam for turning through as shown in fig. 2.

12 cm (4¾ in)

gusset

Fig. 2

5. Clip into the curves and turn through.

6. Stuff the ears lightly and topstitch as shown in fig. 3. Stuff the rest of the body firmly, being especially careful in the neck area. Sew the gap closed.

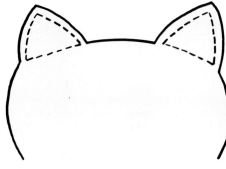

Fig. 3

7. With right sides together, sew the outer seam of the two tail pieces, leaving the straight edge open.

8. Clip into the curves, turn through and stuff firmly.

9. Turn under a small hem at the raw edge and sew the tail to the body above the gusset joint at the rear.

10. On the right side of two back leg pieces – one pointing left and one pointing right – start at the bottom edge and sew lace round close to the raw edge, pleating or gathering the lace round the curves as shown in fig. 4. Repeat for the front legs.

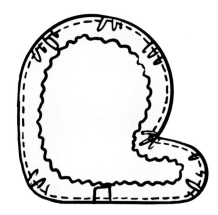

Fig. 4

11. With right sides together, sew the legs in pairs, leaving a gap in the seam as indicated on the pattern.

12. Clip into the curves, turn through and stuff the tops of the legs lightly to the dotted lines as indicated on the pattern. Topstitch across the dotted lines.

13. Stuff the leg bottoms firmly and sew the gaps closed. Catch the legs to the body at the two points on each leg as indicated on the pattern (sew invisibly at the back of legs).

14. To make the bow, fold the fabric in half lengthwise and trim each end as shown in fig. 5.

15. With right sides together, sew the outer seam of the bow, leaving a gap in the centre for turning through as shown in fig. 5.

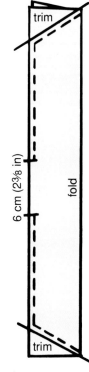

trim

6 cm (2⅜ in)   fold

trim

Fig. 5

16. Turn through and sew the gap closed. Tie the bow round the cat's neck.

Count Snake

This friendly, 182 cm-long (72 in-long) snake is easy to make. He is decorative and educational as children can learn to count to ten on the spots down his back. Either appliqué the felt spots in position or sew on buttons.

REQUIREMENTS

10 pairs 14 cm x 16 cm (5½ in x 6¼ in) body segments in plain fabric.

50 cm x 35 cm (19¾ in x 13¾ in) fabric for head and tail.

polyester stuffing.

two 16 cm (6¼ in) lengths of 8 mm-wide (⅜ in-wide) ribbon.

two bells.

felt or buttons for spots and face.

ribbon for neck.

glue.

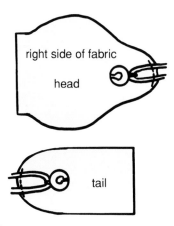

right side of fabric

head

tail

Fig. 1

1. *To make the snake*, transfer the patterns on page 71 onto tracing paper and cut out. Pin the patterns to the fabric and cut out two head and two tail pieces. Cut out the felt spots in the sizes shown on page 71.

2. Thread the bells onto ribbon and sew the raw ends of the ribbon to the right side of one head and one tail piece as shown in fig. 1.

3. Set your sewing machine on a close zig-zag stitch and appliqué the felt spots (alternatively sew on buttons) to one of each pair of body segments as shown in fig. 2 opposite.

4. With right sides together, sew the body segments in sequence. Sew the head piece to segment number one and the tail piece to segment number ten.

5. Sew the underside of the snake's body in the same way and in the same colour sequence.

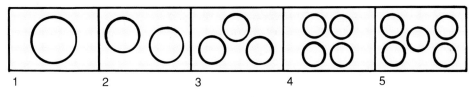
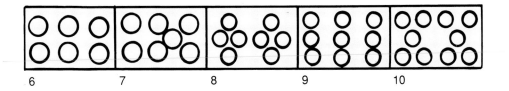

Fig. 2

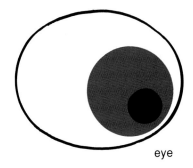
cheek

eye

Fig. 3

6. With right sides together, sew the two body pieces, leaving a gap in the centre, on one side of the body for turning through.

7. Clip into the curves at the neck and turn through. Stuff the snake (not too tightly) and sew the gap closed.

8. Cut the eyes from white, blue and black felt and the heart-shaped cheeks from red felt as shown in fig. 3 and glue them to the snake's head.

9. Using ribbon, tie a bow round the snake's neck.

Unicorn Trophy

This is quite simple to make – the only tricky part is the sewing of the head to the base.

REQUIREMENTS
56 cm x 32 cm (22 in x 12⅝ in)
   fabric for head and ears.
50 cm x 9 cm (19¾ in x 3½ in) of
   same fabric for gusset.
12 cm x 16 cm (4¾ in x 6¼ in)
   contrasting fabric for inner ears.
22 cm x 20 cm (8⅝ in x 7⅞ in)
   white fabric for horn.
scraps of felt for eyes and nose.
wool for mane.
24 cm of 2 cm-wide (9½ in of
   ¾ in-wide) tape for mane.
thin ribbon or cord for wrapping
   round horn.
polyester filling.
black embroidery cotton.
glue.
50 cm (19¾ in) ribbon for neck.
32 cm (12⅝ in) diameter circle
   of firm card.
42 cm (16½ in) diameter circle
   of wadding.
52 cm (20½ in) diameter circle
   of fabric.
strong thread.
18 cm (7 in) diameter circle of felt.
braid for base.
tape or ribbon for hanging loop.

1. **To make the head,** transfer the patterns on pages 90 and 91 onto tracing paper and cut out. Pin the patterns to the fabric and cut out two head pieces, two ear pieces and the gusset. Cut two inner ear pieces from contrasting fabric and the horn from white fabric.

2. Open out the gusset piece and shape one end as indicated on the pattern.

3. With right sides together, sew the ears in pairs, leaving the bottom edge open, and turn through.

4. Fold the ears in half lengthwise and tack across the fold, making a pleat.

5. Sew an ear to the right side of each head piece as shown in fig. 1. Remove the tacking thread from the ears.

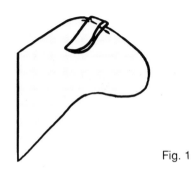

Fig. 1

6. With right sides together, sew the gusset to one head piece with the shaped end of the gusset at the nose end. Trim the excess fabric from the gusset piece at the neck edge.

7. Sew the other head piece to the free edge of the gusset and continue sewing round the outer edge of the head, leaving the neck edge open.

8. Clip into the curves and turn through.

9. Turn under a small hem at the neck edge and sew. Stuff the head firmly.

10. Cut out the eyes as shown in fig. 2 and glue them on. Cut two 1.2 cm x 5 cm (½ in x 2 in) strips of black felt for eyelashes. Cut slits into one long edge of each strip as shown in fig. 3. Glue the un-slit long edge round the eye.

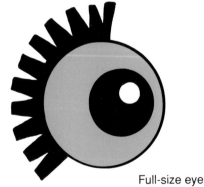

Full-size eye

Fig. 2

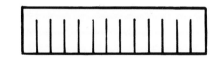

Fig. 3

11. Cut out the nose as shown in fig. 4 and glue it on. Embroider the mouth, taking one long stitch through the snout each time.

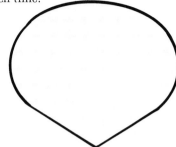

Fig. 4 Full-size nose

12. With right sides together, sew the straight edges of the horn and trim the seam close to the stitching at the point. Turn through and stuff firmly.

13. Turn under and tack a small hem at the bottom edge of the horn. Sew the horn to the head, just above the eyes, in the centre of the gusset.

14. Glue a length of thin ribbon or cord in a spiral round the horn.

15. **To make the base,** apply glue round the outer edge of the card circle and stick it to the centre of the wadding circle.

16. Fold excess wadding over the edge of the card to the back and glue, pleating the wadding slightly.

17. Run a gathering thread round the outer edge of the fabric circle.

18. Padded side down, position the card circle in the centre, on the wrong side of the fabric circle. Pull up gathers tightly, thus enclosing the card base inside the fabric circle, and sew the ends securely.

19. Glue the felt circle on the back of the fabric circle to neaten.

20. Pin and sew the unicorn to the centre of the base. Glue braid round the base of the neck to cover the stitches and round the outer edge of the padded base.

21. **To make the mane,** sew a few stitches down the centre of the tape using a short straight stitch on your sewing machine.

22. Splay the fingers of one hand and wind wool round them to make a thick bunch of loops measuring approximately 10 cm (4 in) across.

23. Slip the wool loops off your fingers, lay them horizontally across the tape and sew through the middle of the loops as shown in fig. 5.

Fig. 5

24. Repeat this procedure, sewing the bunches of wool loops close together, up to approximately 1 cm (⅜ in) from the end of the tape.

25. Cut through all the loops at each side. Turn under the bare ends of the tape at each end and, starting right behind the horn, glue the mane down the centre of the gusset.

26. Sew a loop of ribbon or cord securely to the back of the padded base so that the unicorn can be hung on the wall.

27. Tie a length of ribbon loosely round the neck and make a bow in the front.

Glove Puppets

Some glove puppets are complicated to make, but these glove puppets are quick and easy to make and are ideal for story telling. Create other characters of your own, using this basic shape.

REQUIREMENTS

FOR EACH PUPPET

two 34 cm x 30 cm (13⅜ in x 11¾ in) pieces fabric for body.
felt, buttons, ribbon and wobbly eyes for facial details and features.
glue.
felt-tip pen or embroidery cotton.

1. *To make a puppet,* transfer the pattern on page 92 or 93 onto tracing paper and cut out. Pin the pattern to the fabric and cut out two body pieces on the fold.

2. *To make the frog,* cut two eyes from white felt as indicated on the pattern. Sew the eyes to the right side of the front body piece, using your sewing machine set to a zig-zag stitch.

3. Using a close zig-zag stitch on your sewing machine, embroider the mouth.

4. With right sides together, sew the body back to the body front, leaving the bottom edge open.

5. Clip into the curves and turn through. Turn under and sew a double hem at the bottom edge.

6. Glue on the wobbly eyes or use black felt. Tie a length of ribbon into a bow and glue or sew it to the frog's neck at the centre front.

1. *To make the kitten,* cut two inner ear pieces and the nose from felt as indicated on the pattern and sew to the right side of the front body piece.

2. Embroider the eyes, mouth and whiskers, or use a felt-tip pen.

3. With right sides together, sew the body back to the body front, leaving the bottom edge open.

4. Clip into the curves and turn through. Turn under and sew a double hem at the bottom edge.

5. Using ribbon, tie a bow and glue or sew it to the neck at the centre front.

1. *To make the owl,* cut the eye pieces, beak and chest feathers from felt as indicated on the pattern.

2. Chest feathers are cut from a strip of felt 2.5 cm-wide (1 in-wide). Slit along the long edge and sew to the chest in a curve along the unslit edge.

3. Sew the eye pieces and beak to the right side of the front body piece.

4. With right sides together, sew the body back to the body front, leaving the bottom edge open.

5. Clip into the curves and turn through. Turn under and sew a double hem at the bottom edge.

1. *To make the bear,* cut the muzzle, inner ears and paw pads from felt as indicated on the pattern and sew to the right side of the front body piece.

2. Glue on a black felt nose and add other markings on the muzzle with a black felt-tip pen as indicated on the pattern on page 93.

3. Using a contrast colour cotton, sew a double row of stitching down the centre on the front body piece.

4. With right sides together, sew the body back to the body front, leaving the bottom edge open.

5. Clip into the curves and turn through. Turn under and sew a double hem at the bottom edge.

6. Sew on button eyes and using ribbon, tie a bow and glue or sew it to the neck at the centre front.

7. If desired, make the puppets smaller as shown in fig. 1.

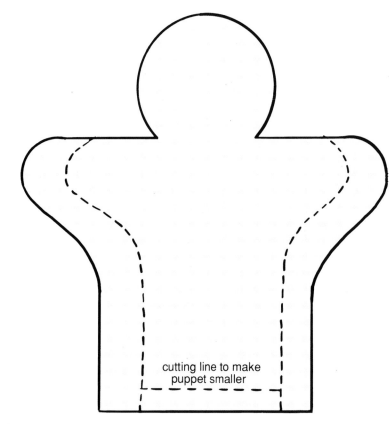

cutting line to make puppet smaller

Fig. 1

Lester Jester

Lester is 20 cm (8 in) from the top of his hat to his chin. This bright boy, covered with bells and ribbons looks super as a wall decoration or as a puppet. Some steps are difficult, but persevere – he's worth the effort!

REQUIREMENTS

22 cm x 42 cm (8⅝ in x 16½ in) flesh-coloured brushed nylon fabric for head.

6 cm (2⅜ in) diameter circle of same flesh-coloured fabric for nose.

30 cm x 30 cm (11¾ in x 11¾ in) fabric for hat.

30 cm x 30 cm (11¾ in x 11¾ in) contrasting fabric for hat.

43 cm x 12 cm (17 in x 4¾ in) fabric for outer frill.

43 cm x 9 cm (17 in x 3½ in) contrasting fabric for inner frill.

two shades of wool for hair (matching the fabric).

three large and a variety of smaller bells for hat and tassles.

a variety of ribbons in different widths for tassles.

1.25 m (49¼ in) ric-rac braid

scraps of black, white and red felt for face.

polyester filling.

red embroidery cotton for mouth.

strong thread.

glue.

1.5 cm (⅝ in) diameter dowel rod.

ribbon for dowel rod (optional).

paint for dowel rod (optional).

1. *To make the head,* transfer the pattern on page 87 onto tracing paper and cut out. Pin the pattern to the fabric and cut out three head pieces.

2. With right sides together, and starting at the neck edge, sew two head pieces along one edge, but only up to the point indicated on the pattern.

3. Sew the third head piece to the free sides of the two joined head pieces, sewing only up to the point indicated on the pattern.

4. Clip into the corners and turn through the gap at the top of the head.

5. Stuff the head firmly, leaving the neck unstuffed, and sew the gap closed. The stuffed head should measure approximately 34 cm (13⅜ in) in diameter.

6. *To make the hat,* transfer the patterns on page 87 onto tracing paper and cut out. Pin the patterns to the fabric and cut out one hat piece from one fabric. Reverse the pattern on the other fabric and cut out the second hat piece.

7. Cut out two identical hat side points from fabric. Reverse the pattern and cut out two identical hat side points from contrasting fabric.

8. With right sides together, sew contrasting pairs of hat side points round the outer edges, leaving the straight edge open. Clip into the curves and turn through. Stuff firmly.

9. With right sides together, sew the two hat pieces, including the darts, as shown in fig. 1.

10. Clip into the curves and turn through. Stuff firmly from the point of the hat to the crown, leaving the crown unstuffed.

11. Position the hat on the head and secure with pins – the centre front of the hat should just cover the sewn gap at the top of the head.

12. Tuck in small amounts of polyester stuffing (use the blunt end of a crochet hook) round the hat to give it a round, even appearance. Sew the hat securely to the head.

13. Turn under a 8 mm (⅜ in) hem at the edge of the hat points. Pin the hat points to the sides of the hat (alternating colours) and sew them neatly in position.

14. Glue a strip of ric-rac braid round the the base of each point, covering the stitching.

15. *To make the nose,* follow the instructions on page 6, using a 6 cm (2⅜ in) diameter circle of fabric. Sew the nose onto the face.

16. *To make the hair,* follow the instructions on page 6, winding the wool round two fingers for the fringe and sides, and round three fingers for the back of the head.

17. Embroider the mouth and glue on the eyes, the mouth centre and the cheeks as shown in fig. 2. Sew bells onto the hat.

18. If desired, paint the dowel rod and wind a length of ribbon round it at an angle. Glue a band of felt round the bottom edge to neaten.

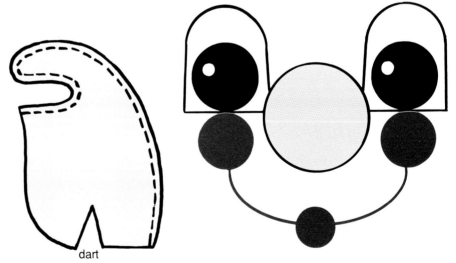

Fig. 1

dart

Fig. 2 Full-size face

19. Push your finger into the head through the neck opening to make a space for the dowel. Push the dowel into the neck and a little way into the head.

20. Using strong thread, tie the head securely to the dowel so that it does not wobble. You can also use glue on the inside of the neck edge to secure the dowel rod.

21. *To make the frills,* cut the fabric strips to the measurements given.

22. With right sides together, sew the short ends of each strip. Turn under and sew a double hem of 6 mm (¼ in) along one raw edge of each circle of fabric. Sew ric-rac braid round the hemmed edges.

23. With right sides facing out, position the wider frill inside the narrower one and, combining the frills, turn under an 8 mm (⅜ in) hem.

24. Run a gathering thread round the neck edge of the combined frill, starting at the centre back seam. Slip the combined frill over the bottom end of the dowel rod, slide it up to the neck position and pull up the gathers tightly. Sew the frill in position round the jester's neck.

25. Using the ribbons, decorate the jester's neck and tie bells onto the ends of the ribbon.

Finger Puppets

Make Snow White and the Seven Dwarfs and enjoy hours of fun. Adapt the pattern for small or big fingers. These can also be made to fit on top of pencils.

REQUIREMENTS
scraps of felt.
1 m (1 yd 3 in) thin cord makes arms for all 10 puppets.
ten pairs of 6 mm (¼ in) diameter wobbly eyes.
seven tiny bells.
gold trimming for prince.
glue.
black felt-tip pen.

1. To make a puppet, transfer the pattern onto tracing paper and cut out. Pin the pattern to the felt and cut out two body pieces.

2. To make the arms, knot cord at one end and cut the cord 4.5 cm (1¾ in) from the knotted end. Position the unknotted end of the cord between the body pieces as indicated on the pattern.

3. Sew the body pieces, using a 4 mm (⅛ in) seam allowance, thus incorporating the arms into the seam.

4. Reinforce the stitching at the beginning and end of the seam.

5. Cut out the face, nose, hair and bow for each finger puppet from felt, as indicated on the pattern, and glue on.

6. Using a black felt-tip pen, mark the facial detail for each puppet as shown on the patterns.

7. Cut a felt beard 2 cm x 1.5 cm-wide (¾ in x ⅝ in-wide) for each dwarf or use the beard patterns given. Slit the beard along one long edge and glue in position.

8. Glue a pink felt nose on each puppet, except the witch, and sew a tiny bell to each dwarf's hat.

9. Glue braid onto the forehead and round the bottom edge of the prince.

10. Glue or sew a red triangular nose to the witch's face.

sew bell here

Dwarfs

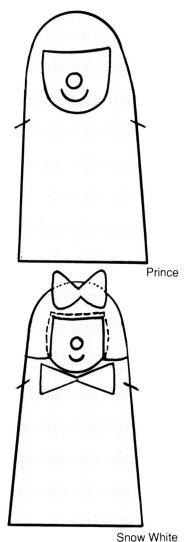

Prince

Beards

Snow White

Witch

Christmas Stocking

The stocking is 40 cm (15¾ in) long and the little pocket on the front can hold an extra gift. Alternatively, tuck in the Father Christmas ornament (see page 61).

1. *To make the stocking,* transfer the pattern on page 94 onto tracing paper and cut out. Pin the pattern to the fabric and cut out two stocking pieces, two heel patches and two toe patches.

2. Sew ric-rac braid to the heel and toe patches as shown in fig. 1.

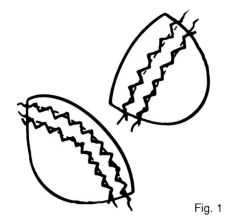

Fig. 1

3. Pin the patches to the right side of each stocking piece and appliqué, using a close zig-zag stitch. It is unnecessary to sew round the outer edge.

4. Turn under and sew a 6 mm (¼ in) double hem along one edge of the pocket and turn under a small hem on the other three sides.

5. Pin the pocket in position on the right side of the stocking front and sew.

6. With right sides together, sew the stocking pieces along the outer edges, leaving the top edge open.

7. Fold a 20 cm (7⅞ in) length of ribbon in half to form a loop and sew the raw ends of the loop to the wrong side of the back seam of the stocking, as shown in fig. 2.

Fig. 2

8. With right sides together, sew the short edges of the collar to form a circle.

9. With wrong sides together, fold the collar piece in half lengthwise, aligning the raw edges.

10. Match the seam in the collar piece to the back seam of the stocking and pin the collar to the wrong side of the stocking all round the top edge.

11. Use a 1 cm (⅜ in) seam allowance and sew the collar to the stocking, incorporating the raw ends of the ribbon into the seam. Turn through.

12. Fold the collar over to the front of the stocking along the seam line and press in position.

13. Sew on a length of ribbon round the collar. Using ribbon, tie a bow and sew it to the ribbon round the collar at the centre front of the stocking.

Festive Birds

These Christmas tree decorations also make a lovely mobile, suspended from ribbons of different lengths and colours.

REQUIREMENTS
FOR EACH BIRD
scraps of fabric.
polyester filling.
ric-rac, braid and ribbon.
glue.
sequins or embroidery cotton
   for eyes.
tiny bell.

1. *To make a bird*, transfer the patterns on page 95 onto tracing paper and cut out. Pin the patterns to the fabric and cut out two body and four wing pieces.

2. On the right side of each body piece, decorate the tail with ric-rac, braid or ribbon and sew in position.

3. With right sides together, sew the body pieces, leaving a gap for turning through.

4. With right sides together, sew the wings in pairs, remembering to leave a gap for turning through.

5. Clip into the curves of the body and wings and turn through.

6. Stuff the body firmly and the wings lightly with polyester filling.

7. Sew the gaps closed and sew a loop of ribbon (or cord) to the top inner corner of the tail, as indicated on the pattern, for hanging.

8. Glue or sew a piece of braid round the body at the start of the tail and tie a ribbon round the neck, enclosing a tiny bell into the knot as shown in fig. 1.

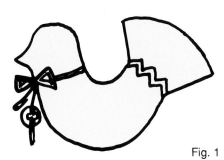

Fig. 1

9. Glue the wings in position on each side of the body and glue a sequin, or embroider an eye, on each side of the bird's head.

Christmas Stars

You can make the stars without the faces. Decorate with felt holly leaves and berries or sparkling braids.

REQUIREMENTS
FOR EACH STAR
two 16 cm x 16 cm (6¼ in x 6¼ in)
  pieces fabric for star.
6 cm (2⅜ in) diameter circle of
  flesh-coloured fabric (with stretch).
polyester filling.
red and black felt for eyes and nose.
ribbon.
red embroidery cotton.
powder rouge.
wool for hair.
five tiny bells.
glue.

1. *To make the star,* transfer the pattern on page 95 onto tracing paper and cut out. Pin the pattern to the fabric and cut out one front on the fold and two backs.

2. With right sides together, sew the back pieces down the centre back seam, leaving a gap for turning through.

3. Sew a loop of ribbon to the right side of the top point of the star front piece, as shown in fig. 1.

right side

Fig. 1

4. With right sides together, sew the star back and front round the outer edge, leaving a gap for turning through.

5. Clip into the corners, turn through and stuff firmly. Sew the gap closed.

6. *To make the face,* run a gathering thread round the outer edge of the flesh-coloured fabric circle. Put a ball of stuffing into the centre of the circle, pull up the gathers and sew the ends securely to form the head. Sew the head to the centre front of the star.

7. *To make the hair,* wind wool round three fingers ten times. Slip the loops off your fingers, tie a piece of wool tightly round the middle and trim the loops at each side. Sew or glue the centre of the hair to the centre of the forehead.

8. Cut two small, black felt circles for the eyes and one small, red felt circle for the nose and glue in position. Embroider a couple of small, straight stitches for the mouth and rouge the cheeks.

9. Tie a length of ribbon into a bow and glue it under the chin.

10. Sew a bell to each point of the star.

Father Christmas

Each Father Christmas is 16 cm (6¼ in) tall. Make about six to hang on the Christmas tree. Using the same basic pattern, but changing the colours, try making some elves too.

REQUIREMENTS

FOR EACH FATHER CHRISTMAS

**13 cm x 36 cm (5⅛ in x 14¼ in)
red fabric.**
**7 cm x 36 cm (2¾ in x 14¼ in)
flesh-coloured fabric.**
polyester filling.
glue.
red felt for hat.
scraps of white fake fur or felt.
felt or thin vinyl-type fabric for belt.
red felt-tip pen.
ribbon for hanging.
**scraps of black and pink felt for the
eyes and nose.**

1. To make the Father Christmas, transfer the pattern on page 95 onto tracing paper and cut out.

2. With right sides together, sew the flesh-coloured fabric to the red fabric along one long edge, using an 8 mm (⅜ in) seam. Press the seam allowance to the side of the red fabric.

3. With right sides together, fold the joined fabric in half, short edges together and matching the seam line (between the flesh-coloured and red fabric).

4. Pin the pattern to the wrong side of the folded fabric, with the neckline on the pattern aligned with the join of the two fabrics. Trace round the pattern as shown in fig. 1.

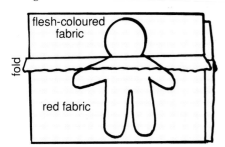

Fig. 1

5. Sew round the traced line, leaving a gap at the top for turning through.

6. Cut out the body, leaving a 3 mm (⅛ in) seam allowance, except between the legs where you'll have to be very careful.

7. Clip carefully into the corners, turn through and stuff. Sew the gap closed.

8. To make the hat, transfer the pattern on page 95 onto tracing paper and cut out. Pin the traced pattern to the red felt and cut out the hat.

9. With right sides together, sew the side seam to make a cone. Turn through and push the hat point out carefully.

10. Glue the hat to Father Christmas's head and glue a thin strip of fake fur (or white felt) round the hat edge, round the wrists, and round the body above the top of the legs.

11. To make the beard, transfer the pattern on page 95 onto tracing paper and cut out. Pin the pattern to white felt and cut out the beard.

12. Glue the beard onto the face and colour the mouth with a red felt-tip pen. Glue on a small pink circle of felt for the nose and small black circles of felt for the eyes. Using white paint, add a dot to each eye.

13. Cut an 8 mm-wide (⅜ in-wide) length of black vinyl (or felt) for a belt. Glue the belt round the waist and join it at the centre front. Glue a felt buckle over the join.

14. Using ribbon, sew a loop to the top of the head for hanging.

Christmas Angel

The angel is 34 cm (13 in) tall and makes a lovely centrepiece on the Christmas table, or at the centre of the mantelpiece.
Use anglaise edging for the clothing and wings, trimming off the raw edge to achieve the desired width. If you use other fabric, allow extra for a hem. There is no pattern.

REQUIREMENTS

12 cm (4¾ in) diameter circle of firm cardboard.
26 cm x 38 cm (10¼ in x 15 in) white fabric for body.
18 cm (7 in) diameter circle of the same fabric.
17.5 cm x 24 cm (6⅞ in x 9½ in) stretch fabric for head.
two 17 cm x 6 cm (6¾ in x 2⅜ in) pieces stretch fabric for arms.
1 m of 27 cm-wide (1 yd 3 in of 10⅝ in-wide) anglaise edging for dress.
two 22.5 cm (8⅞ in) pieces of 13.5 cm-wide (5⅜ in-wide) anglaise edging for sleeves.
61 cm of 12 cm-wide (24 in of 4¾ in-wide) anglaise edging for wings.
polyester filling.
a small weight.
strong thread.
10 cm of 1.5 cm (4 in of ⅝ in) diameter dowel rod.
wool for hair (mohair).
pre-gathered lace for neck.
1 m of 1.5 cm-wide (1 yd 3 in of ⅝ in-wide) ribbon for waist.
scrap of narrow ribbon or cord to tie wings.
scraps of silver ric-rac, braid, ribbon or cord.
scraps of black and dark pink felt for eyes and mouth.
powder rouge.
glue.
metal star-shaped studs and cord to hang from hands (optional).

1. *To make the head*, with right sides together, sew the two short edges of the stretch fabric for the head to form a tube.

2. Run a gathering thread along one raw edge, pull up the gathers tightly and sew the ends securely to make the top of the angel's head.

3. Turn through and mark a line 8 cm (3¼ in) from the bottom raw edge. Stuff the head firmly up to the mark.

4. Run a gathering thread round the head tube at the 8 cm (3¼ in) mark and push one end of the dowel into the head cavity. Pull up the gathers tightly round the dowel and sew the ends securely.

5. Wrap a length of strong thread round the rest of the dowel rod, enclosing the rest of the head fabric, thus forming a neck as shown in fig. 1.

Fig. 1

6. *To make the body*, run a gathering thread round the circle of fabric.

7. Put the cardboard circle in the centre, on the wrong side of the fabric circle, and pull up the gathers tightly to enclose the cardboard. Sew the ends securely.

8. With right sides together, sew the two short edges of the body piece to form a tube, and turn through.

9. Turn under and hem one raw edge of the body piece. Sew the tube round the bottom hemmed edge to the covered base. Thinly stuff the base, put in the weight and continue stuffing round the weight up to the raw edge of the body.

10. Run a gathering thread round the raw edge and push the neck into the body. Pull up the gathers tightly round the dowel and sew round the neck securely. Don't worry if it looks untidy since it will be covered later.

11. *To make the arms*, sew and trim the fabric as shown in fig. 2. Turn through and stuff the arms, leaving the top 3 cm (1¼ in) unstuffed.

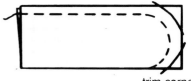

Fig. 2   trim corners

12. Turn under the raw edge of each arm and sew the arms to each side of the body at shoulder level.

13. *To make the dress*, cut the anglaise in half, so that you have two pieces each 50 cm x 27 cm (20 in x 10⅝ in).

14. With right sides together, sew the shoulder seams for 3 cm (1¼ in) on each side, as shown in fig. 3.

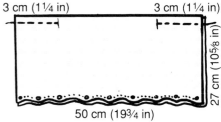

3 cm (1¼ in)   3 cm (1¼ in)

27 cm (10⅝ in)

50 cm (19¾ in)

Fig. 3

15. With right sides together, sew the sleeves to the dress as shown in fig. 4.

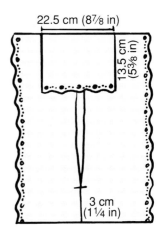

22.5 cm (8⅞ in)

13.5 cm (5⅜ in)

3 cm (1¼ in)

Fig. 4

16. With right sides together, sew the underarm seams from each wrist to the bottom edge of the dress.

17. Clip into the underarm corners and turn through. Turn under a small hem at the neck edge and, starting at the centre of the dress back, run a gathering thread round the neck edge.

18. Put the dress on the body, pull up the gathers tightly round the neck and sew the ends securely.

19. Sew the pre-gathered lace round the angel's neck.

20. *To make the hair,* follow the instructions on page 6 and wrap the wool round one finger. Cover the head with curls.

21. Tie a piece of silver ric-rac or braid round the forehead, tying a knot at the back of the head.

22. *To make the face,* follow the instructions on page 7 and use a 2.5 cm (1 in) diameter circle of flesh-coloured fabric. Sew or glue the nose to the face.

23. Cut a small oval from dark pink felt for the mouth and glue it in position on the angel's face.

24. Cut two small circles of black felt for the eyes and glue them in position. Rouge the cheeks.

25. *To make the wings,* with right sides together, sew the short edges of the fabric and turn through.

26. Turn under a 6 mm (¼ in) double hem along the raw edge (the other edge is the scalloped edge of anglaise).

27. Position the seam to the centre back as shown in fig. 5.

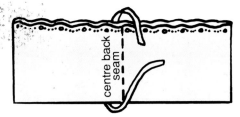

Fig. 5

28. Tie narrow ribbon or cord round the fabric at the centre, making a bow tie as shown in fig. 6.

Fig. 6

1.5 cm (⅝ in)

29. Mark the centre of the wide ribbon for the waist and sew it to the centre back of the narrow ribbon or cord round the angel's wings.

30. Bring the long ends of the ribbon round the waist and tie in a bow at the centre front, positioning the wings centrally at the back.

> **NOTE:** *Three star-shaped studs can be fixed onto a length of silver ric-rac or braid, and sewn onto the angel's hands.*

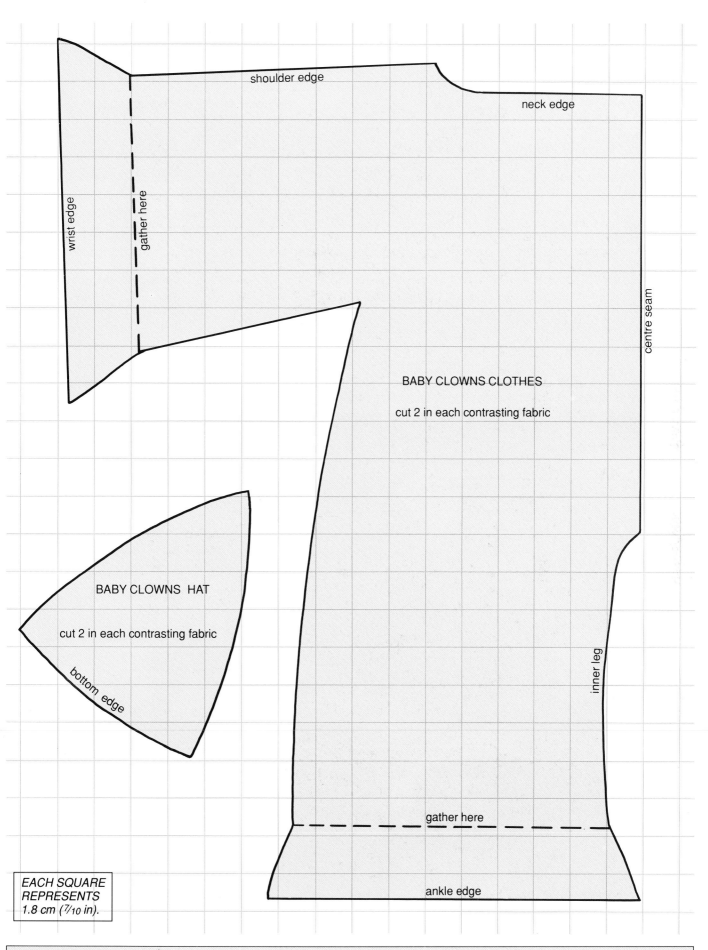

shoulder edge

neck edge

wrist edge

gather here

centre seam

BABY CLOWNS CLOTHES

cut 2 in each contrasting fabric

BABY CLOWNS HAT

cut 2 in each contrasting fabric

bottom edge

inner leg

gather here

ankle edge

EACH SQUARE
REPRESENTS
1.8 cm (⁷/₁₀ in).

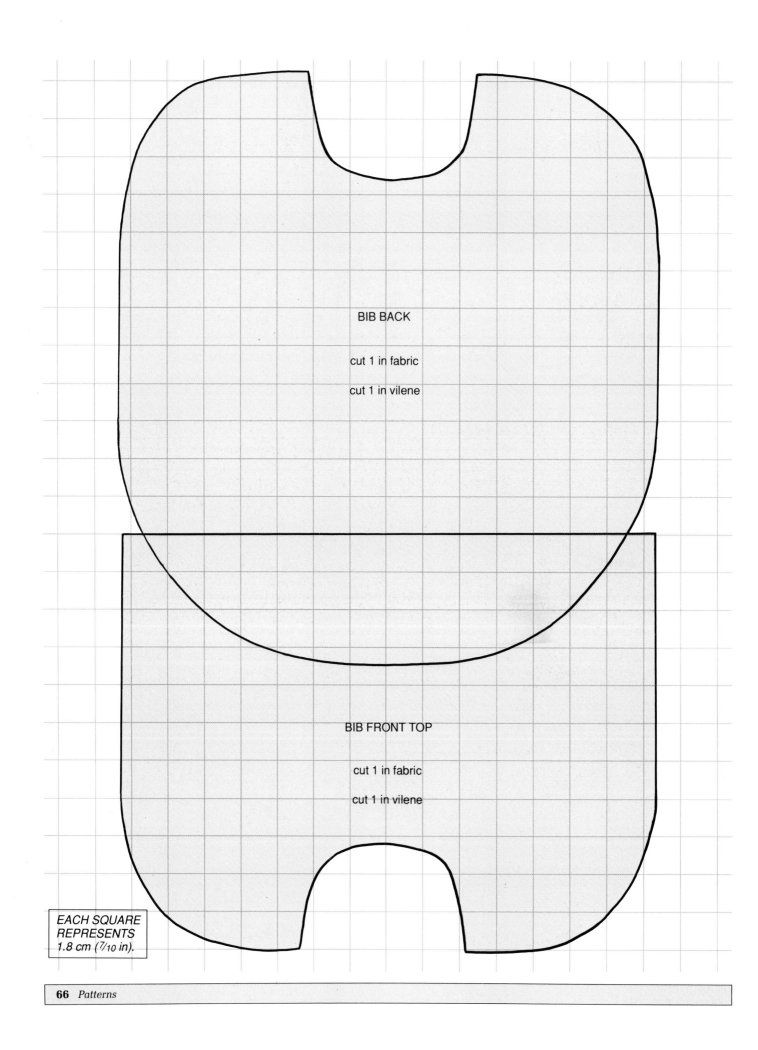

BIB BACK

cut 1 in fabric

cut 1 in vilene

BIB FRONT TOP

cut 1 in fabric

cut 1 in vilene

EACH SQUARE
REPRESENTS
1.8 cm (7/10 in).

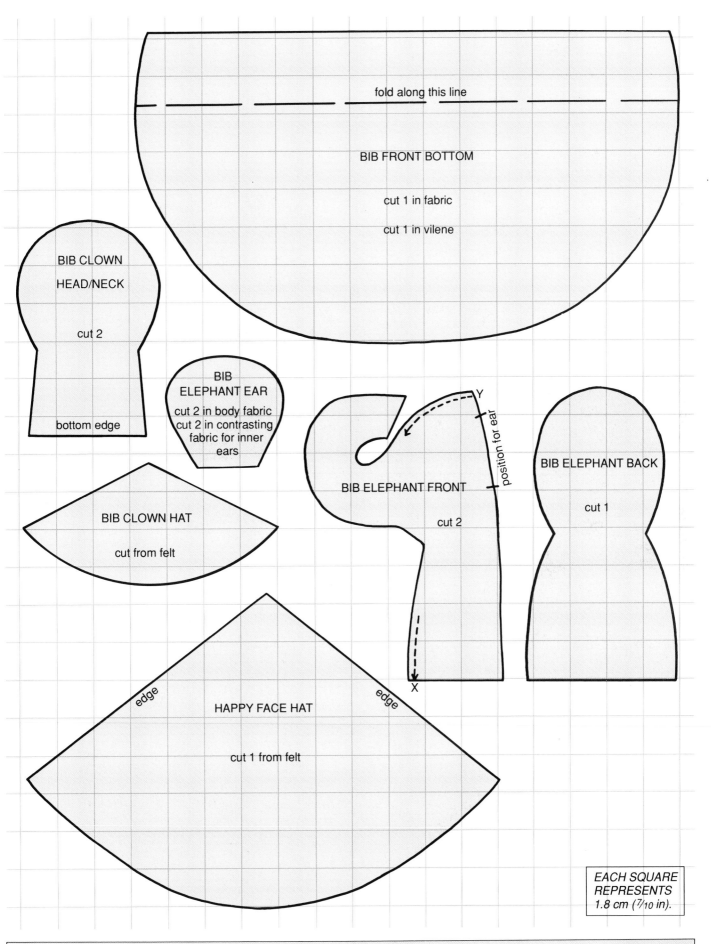

fold along this line

BIB FRONT BOTTOM

cut 1 in fabric

cut 1 in vilene

BIB CLOWN
HEAD/NECK

cut 2

bottom edge

BIB
ELEPHANT EAR

cut 2 in body fabric
cut 2 in contrasting
fabric for inner
ears

BIB CLOWN HAT

cut from felt

BIB ELEPHANT FRONT

cut 2

Y

position for ear

X

BIB ELEPHANT BACK

cut 1

edge

edge

HAPPY FACE HAT

cut 1 from felt

EACH SQUARE
REPRESENTS
1.8 cm (7/10 in).

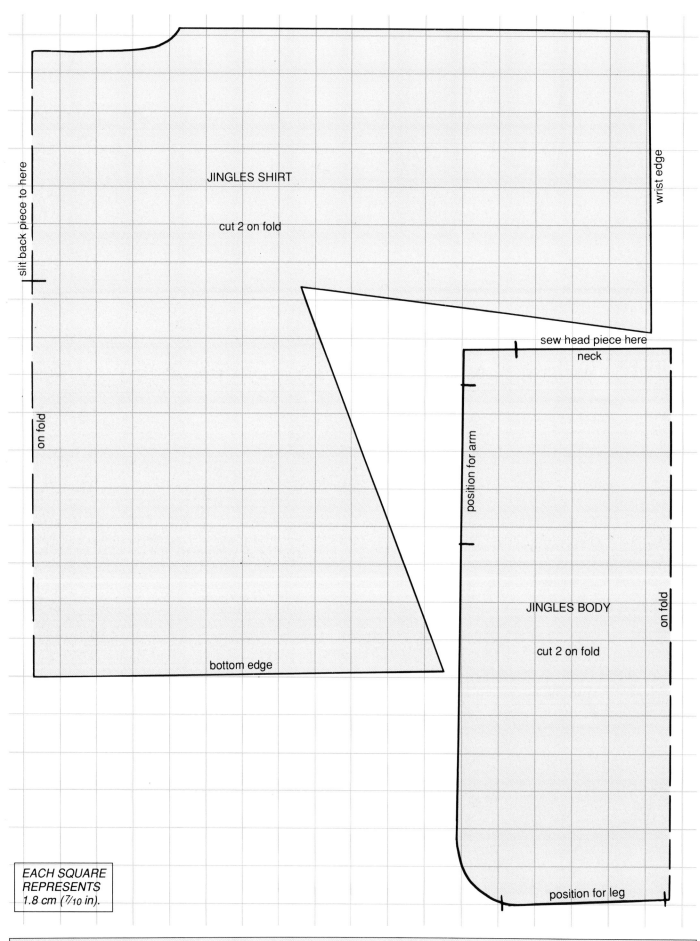

JINGLES SHIRT

cut 2 on fold

slit back piece to here

wrist edge

on fold

bottom edge

sew head piece here

neck

position for arm

JINGLES BODY

cut 2 on fold

on fold

position for leg

EACH SQUARE
REPRESENTS
1.8 cm (7/10 in).

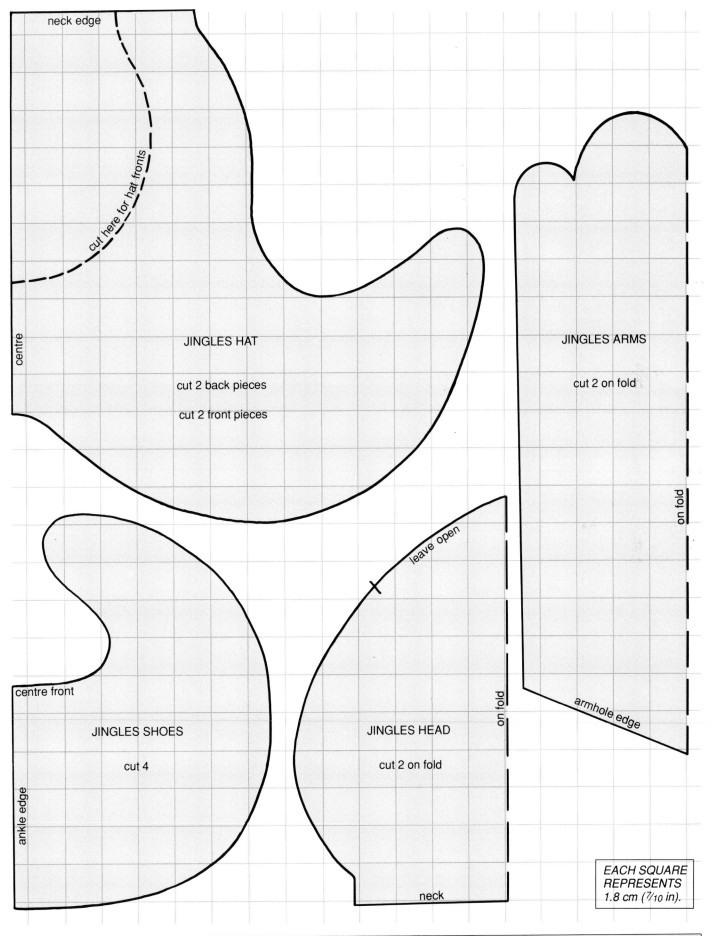

neck edge

cut here for hat fronts

centre

JINGLES HAT

cut 2 back pieces

cut 2 front pieces

JINGLES ARMS

cut 2 on fold

on fold

leave open

centre front

JINGLES SHOES

cut 4

ankle edge

on fold

JINGLES HEAD

cut 2 on fold

neck

armhole edge

*EACH SQUARE
REPRESENTS
1.8 cm (⁷/₁₀ in).*

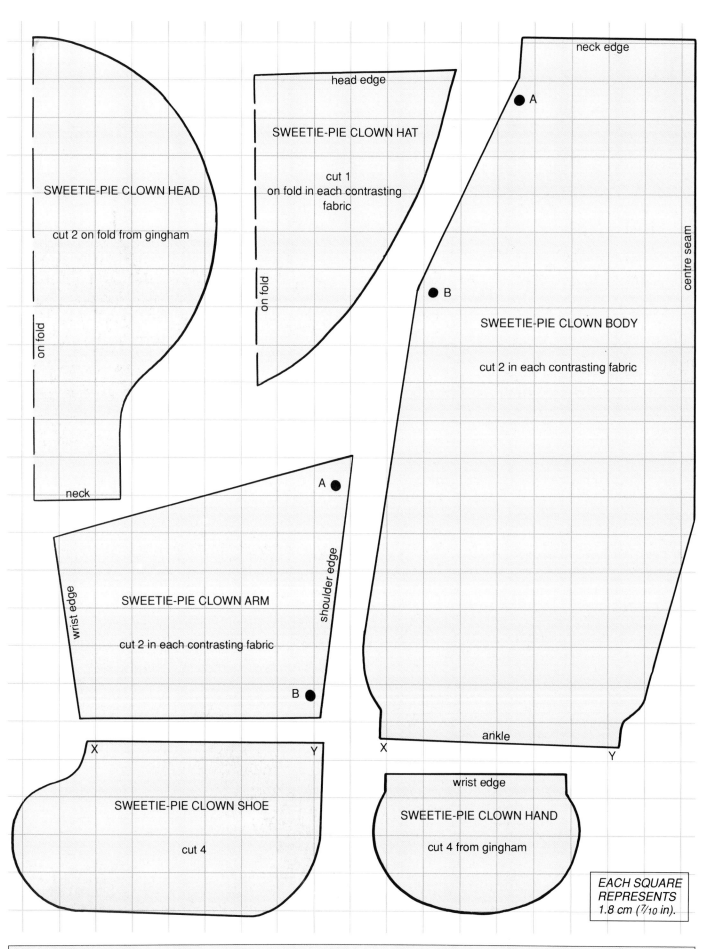

SWEETIE-PIE CLOWN HEAD

cut 2 on fold from gingham

on fold

neck

SWEETIE-PIE CLOWN HAT

cut 1
on fold in each contrasting
fabric

head edge

on fold

neck edge

● A

● B

centre seam

SWEETIE-PIE CLOWN BODY

cut 2 in each contrasting fabric

A ●

shoulder edge

wrist edge

SWEETIE-PIE CLOWN ARM

cut 2 in each contrasting fabric

B ●

X   Y

ankle

X   Y

X   Y

SWEETIE-PIE CLOWN SHOE

cut 4

wrist edge

SWEETIE-PIE CLOWN HAND

cut 4 from gingham

EACH SQUARE
REPRESENTS
1.8 cm (7/10 in).

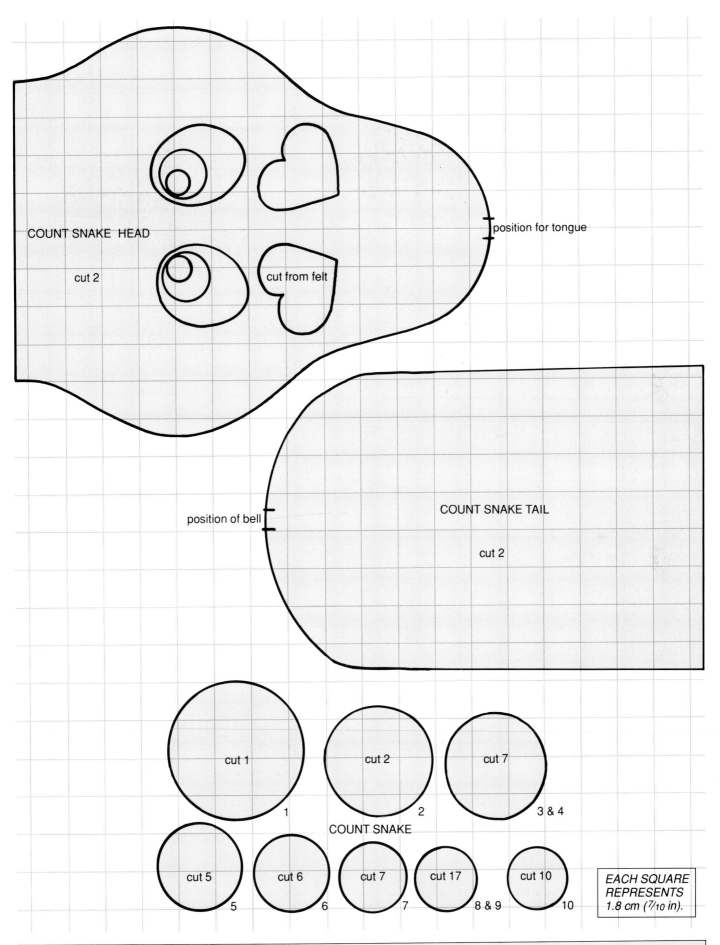

COUNT SNAKE HEAD

cut 2

cut from felt

position for tongue

position of bell

COUNT SNAKE TAIL

cut 2

cut 1

cut 2

cut 7

1

2

3 & 4

COUNT SNAKE

cut 5

cut 6

cut 7

cut 17

cut 10

5

6

7

8 & 9

10

*EACH SQUARE
REPRESENTS
1.8 cm (7/10 in).*

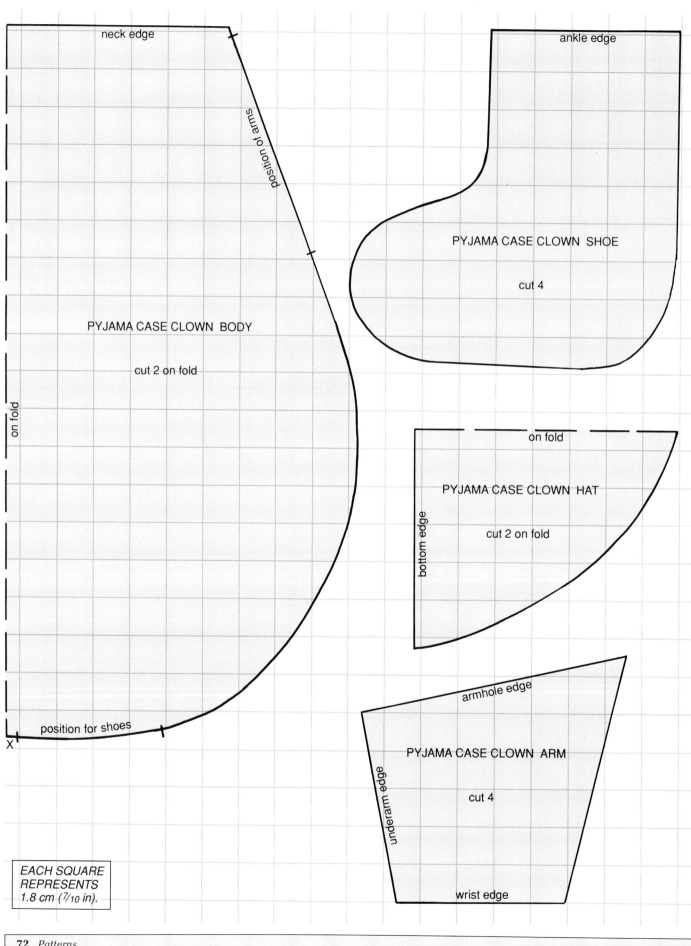

neck edge

position of arms

PYJAMA CASE CLOWN BODY

cut 2 on fold

on fold

position for shoes

X

ankle edge

PYJAMA CASE CLOWN SHOE

cut 4

on fold

PYJAMA CASE CLOWN HAT

cut 2 on fold

bottom edge

armhole edge

PYJAMA CASE CLOWN ARM

cut 4

underarm edge

wrist edge

EACH SQUARE
REPRESENTS
1.8 cm (⁷/₁₀ in).

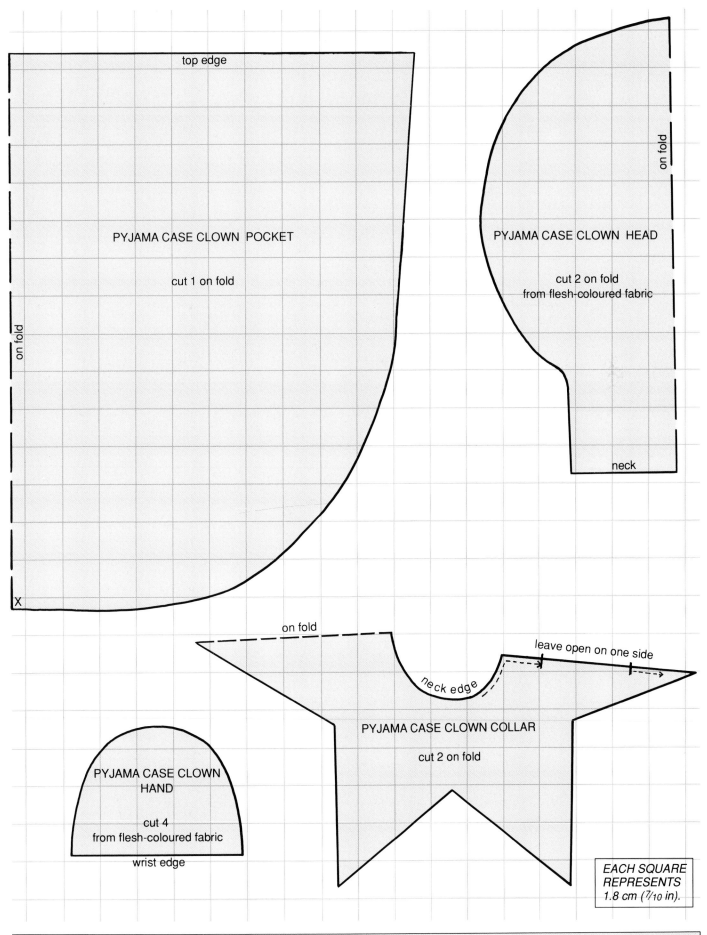

top edge

on fold

PYJAMA CASE CLOWN POCKET

cut 1 on fold

X

on fold

PYJAMA CASE CLOWN HEAD

cut 2 on fold
from flesh-coloured fabric

neck

on fold

neck edge

leave open on one side

PYJAMA CASE CLOWN COLLAR

cut 2 on fold

PYJAMA CASE CLOWN
HAND

cut 4
from flesh-coloured fabric

wrist edge

EACH SQUARE
REPRESENTS
1.8 cm (7/10 in).

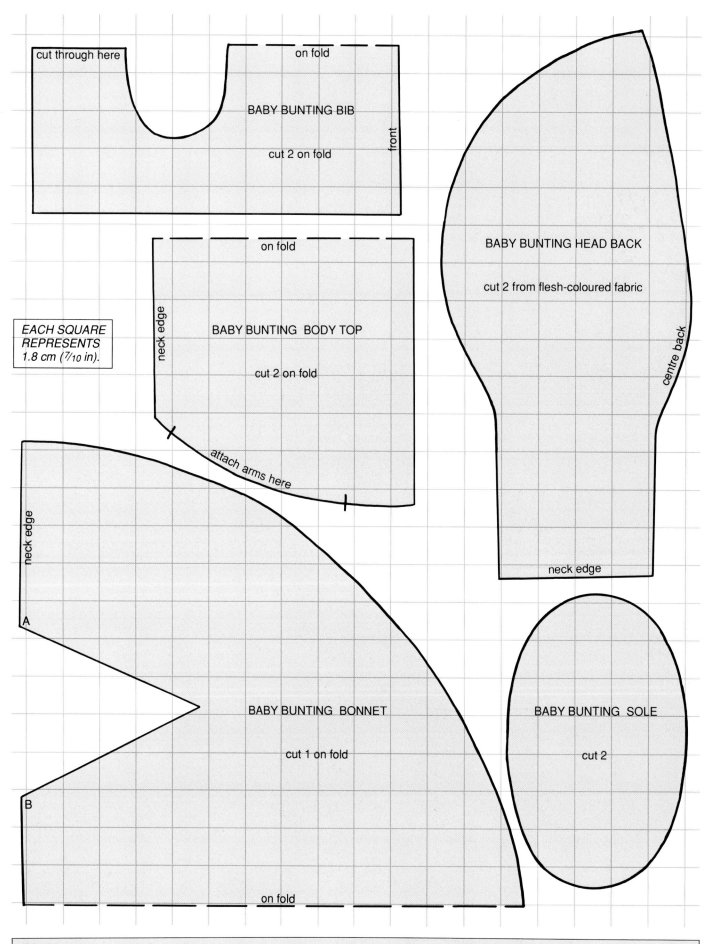

cut through here

on fold

BABY BUNTING BIB

cut 2 on fold

front

BABY BUNTING HEAD BACK

cut 2 from flesh-coloured fabric

centre back

EACH SQUARE
REPRESENTS
1.8 cm (7/10 in).

on fold

neck edge

BABY BUNTING BODY TOP

cut 2 on fold

attach arms here

neck edge

neck edge

A

B

BABY BUNTING BONNET

cut 1 on fold

BABY BUNTING SOLE

cut 2

on fold

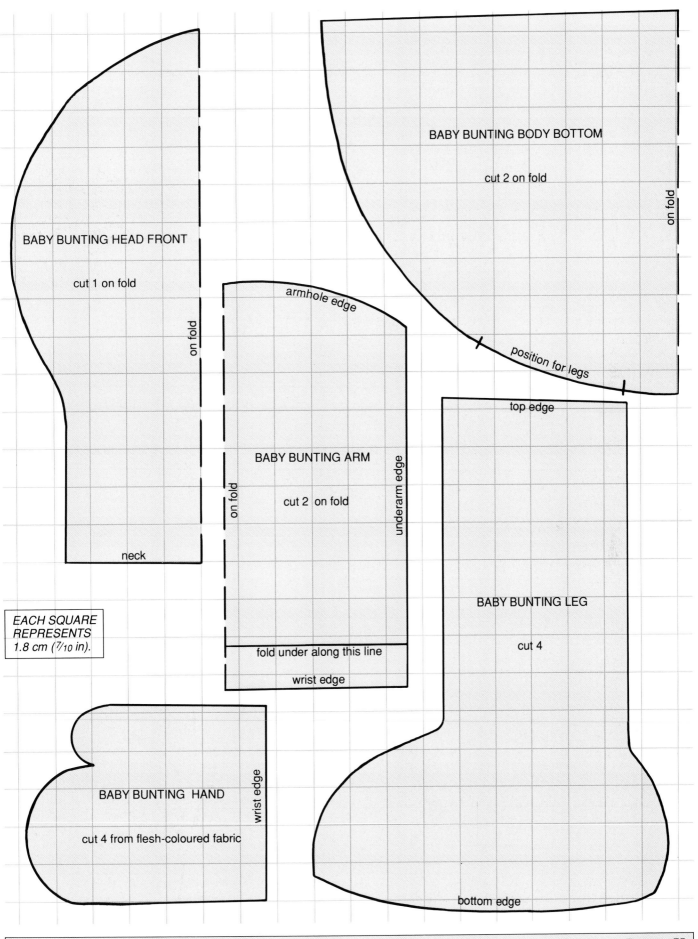

BABY BUNTING HEAD FRONT

cut 1 on fold

on fold

neck

BABY BUNTING BODY BOTTOM

cut 2 on fold

on fold

position for legs

armhole edge

BABY BUNTING ARM

cut 2 on fold

on fold

underarm edge

fold under along this line

wrist edge

top edge

BABY BUNTING LEG

cut 4

bottom edge

EACH SQUARE
REPRESENTS
1.8 cm (7/10 in).

BABY BUNTING HAND

cut 4 from flesh-coloured fabric

wrist edge

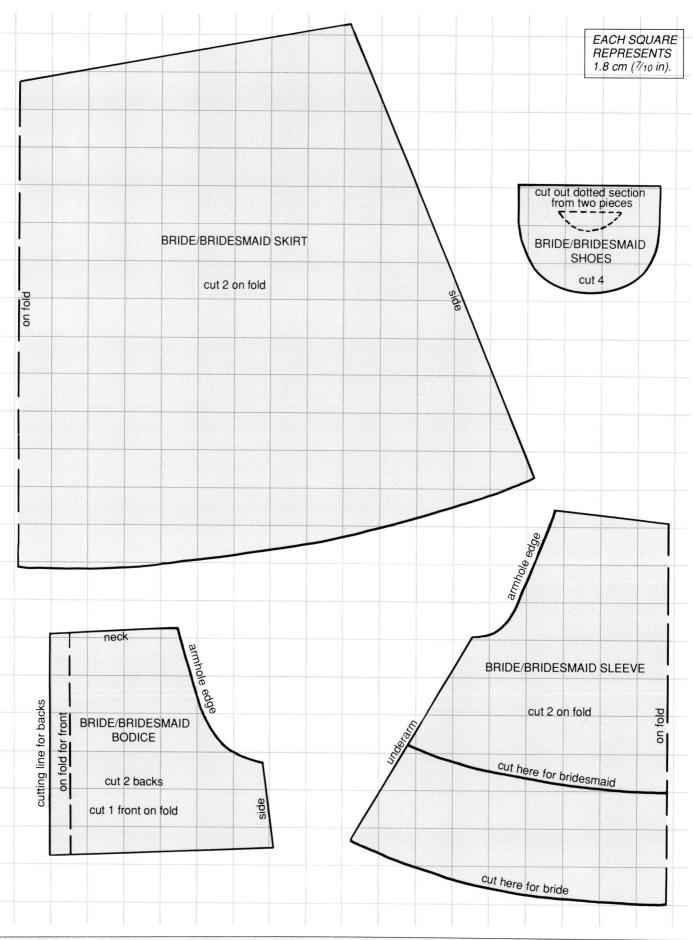

EACH SQUARE REPRESENTS 1.8 cm (⁷/₁₀ in).

BRIDE/BRIDESMAID SKIRT

cut 2 on fold

on fold

side

cut out dotted section from two pieces

BRIDE/BRIDESMAID SHOES

cut 4

armhole edge

BRIDE/BRIDESMAID SLEEVE

cut 2 on fold

on fold

underarm

cut here for bridesmaid

cut here for bride

neck

armhole edge

cutting line for backs

on fold for front

BRIDE/BRIDESMAID BODICE

cut 2 backs

cut 1 front on fold

side

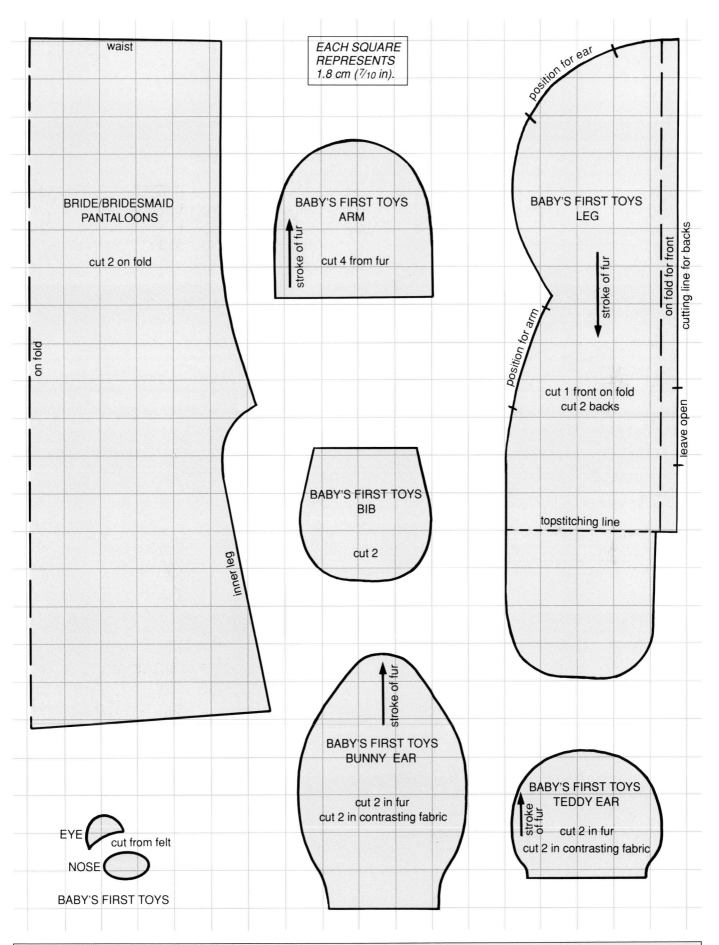

waist

BRIDE/BRIDESMAID
PANTALOONS

cut 2 on fold

on fold

inner leg

EACH SQUARE
REPRESENTS
1.8 cm (7/10 in).

BABY'S FIRST TOYS
ARM

stroke of fur

cut 4 from fur

BABY'S FIRST TOYS
BIB

cut 2

position for ear

BABY'S FIRST TOYS
LEG

stroke of fur

position for arm

on fold for front

cutting line for backs

cut 1 front on fold
cut 2 backs

leave open

topstitching line

BABY'S FIRST TOYS
BUNNY EAR

stroke of fur

cut 2 in fur
cut 2 in contrasting fabric

BABY'S FIRST TOYS
TEDDY EAR

stroke of fur

cut 2 in fur
cut 2 in contrasting fabric

EYE

cut from felt

NOSE

BABY'S FIRST TOYS

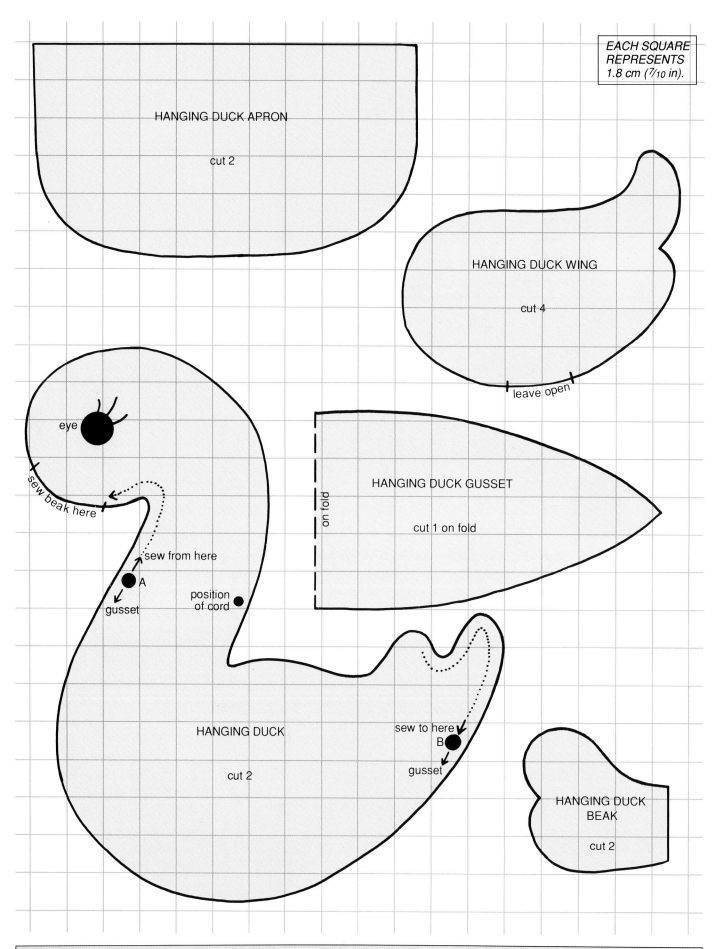

EACH SQUARE
REPRESENTS
1.8 cm (⁷/10 in).

HANGING DUCK APRON

cut 2

HANGING DUCK WING

cut 4

leave open

eye

sew beak here

sew from here

A

gusset

position
of cord

HANGING DUCK GUSSET

on fold

cut 1 on fold

sew to here

B

gusset

HANGING DUCK

cut 2

HANGING DUCK
BEAK

cut 2

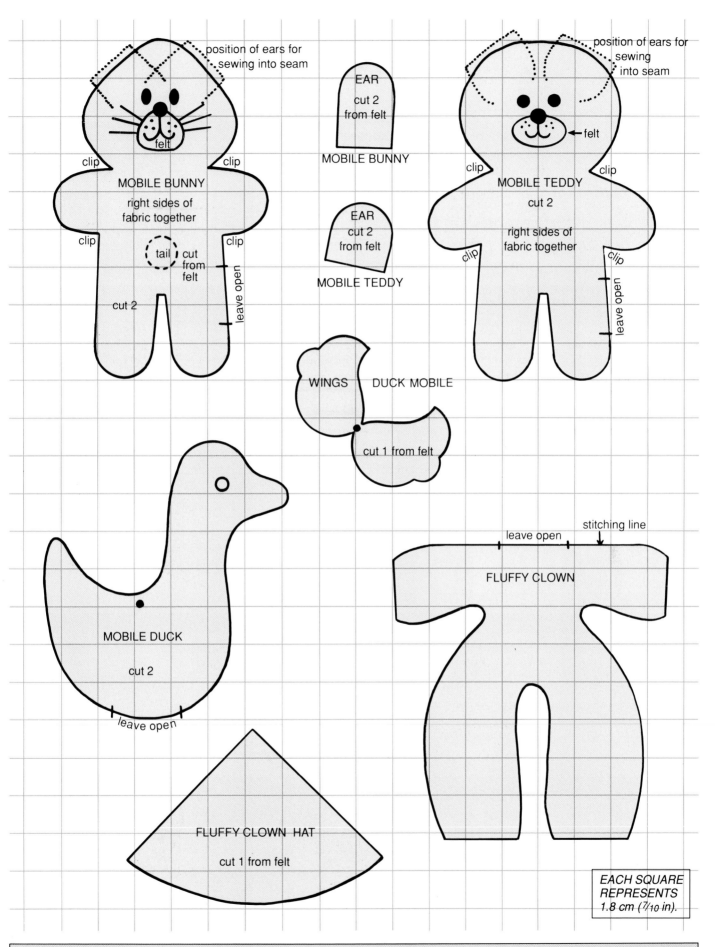

position of ears for
sewing into seam

EAR
cut 2
from felt

MOBILE BUNNY

clip

clip

MOBILE BUNNY

right sides of
fabric together

tail cut
from
felt

cut 2

leave open

EAR
cut 2
from felt

MOBILE TEDDY

position of ears for
sewing into seam

felt

clip

clip

MOBILE TEDDY

cut 2

right sides of
fabric together

clip

clip

leave open

WINGS   DUCK MOBILE

cut 1 from felt

leave open   stitching line

FLUFFY CLOWN

MOBILE DUCK

cut 2

leave open

FLUFFY CLOWN HAT

cut 1 from felt

EACH SQUARE
REPRESENTS
1.8 cm (7/10 in).

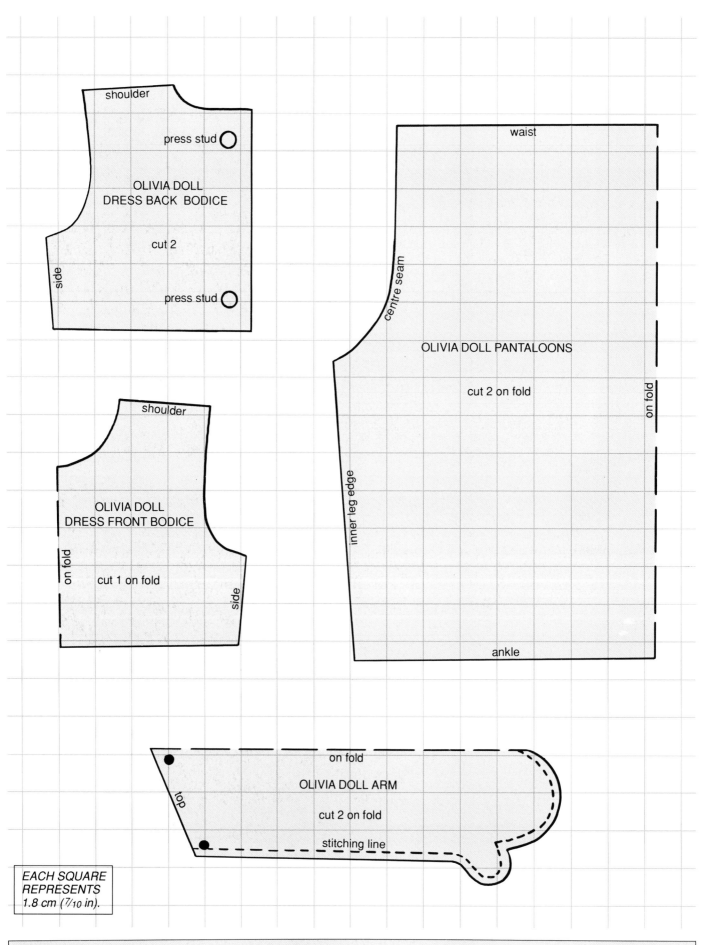

shoulder

press stud ◯

OLIVIA DOLL
DRESS BACK BODICE

cut 2

press stud ◯

side

waist

centre seam

OLIVIA DOLL PANTALOONS

cut 2 on fold

on fold

inner leg edge

ankle

shoulder

OLIVIA DOLL
DRESS FRONT BODICE

on fold

cut 1 on fold

side

on fold

OLIVIA DOLL ARM

top

cut 2 on fold

stitching line

EACH SQUARE
REPRESENTS
1.8 cm (⁷/₁₀ in).

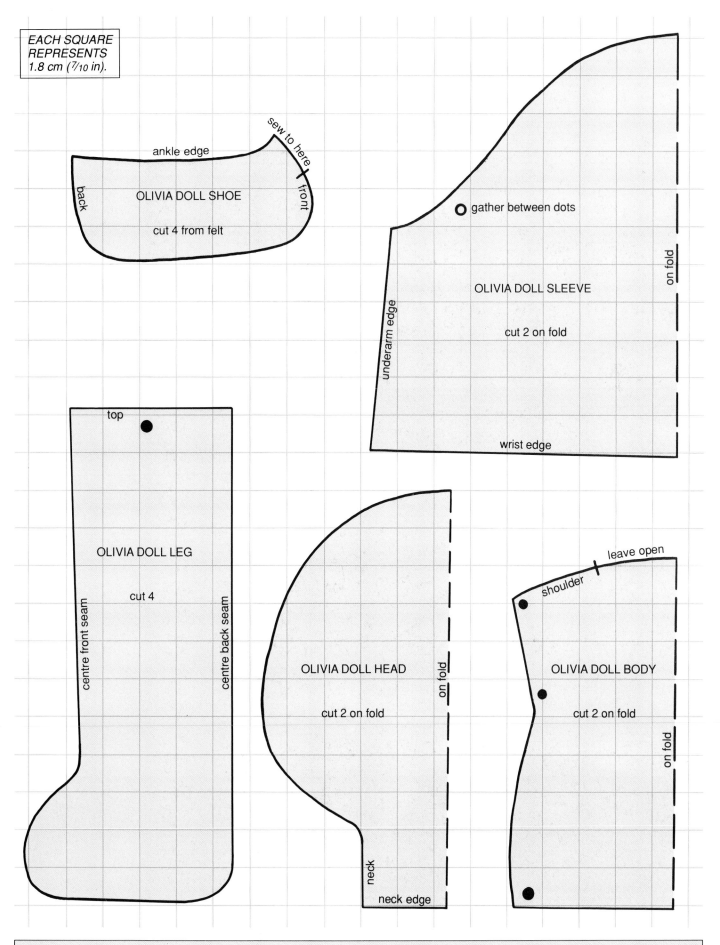

EACH SQUARE
REPRESENTS
1.8 cm (⁷/₁₀ in).

ankle edge

sew to here

back

OLIVIA DOLL SHOE

front

cut 4 from felt

○ gather between dots

underarm edge

OLIVIA DOLL SLEEVE

on fold

cut 2 on fold

wrist edge

top ●

OLIVIA DOLL LEG

cut 4

centre front seam

centre back seam

leave open

shoulder

OLIVIA DOLL HEAD

on fold

cut 2 on fold

OLIVIA DOLL BODY

cut 2 on fold

on fold

neck

neck edge

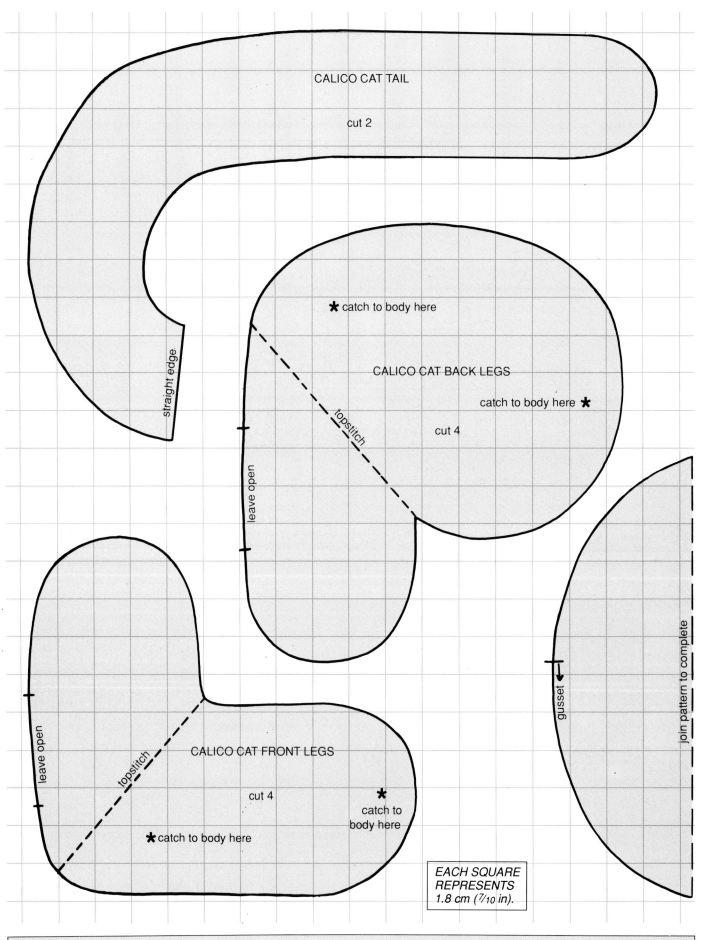

CALICO CAT TAIL

cut 2

straight edge

* catch to body here

CALICO CAT BACK LEGS

catch to body here *

cut 4

topstitch

leave open

gusset

join pattern to complete

leave open

topstitch

CALICO CAT FRONT LEGS

cut 4

*
catch to
body here

* catch to body here

EACH SQUARE
REPRESENTS
1.8 cm (⁷⁄₁₀ in).

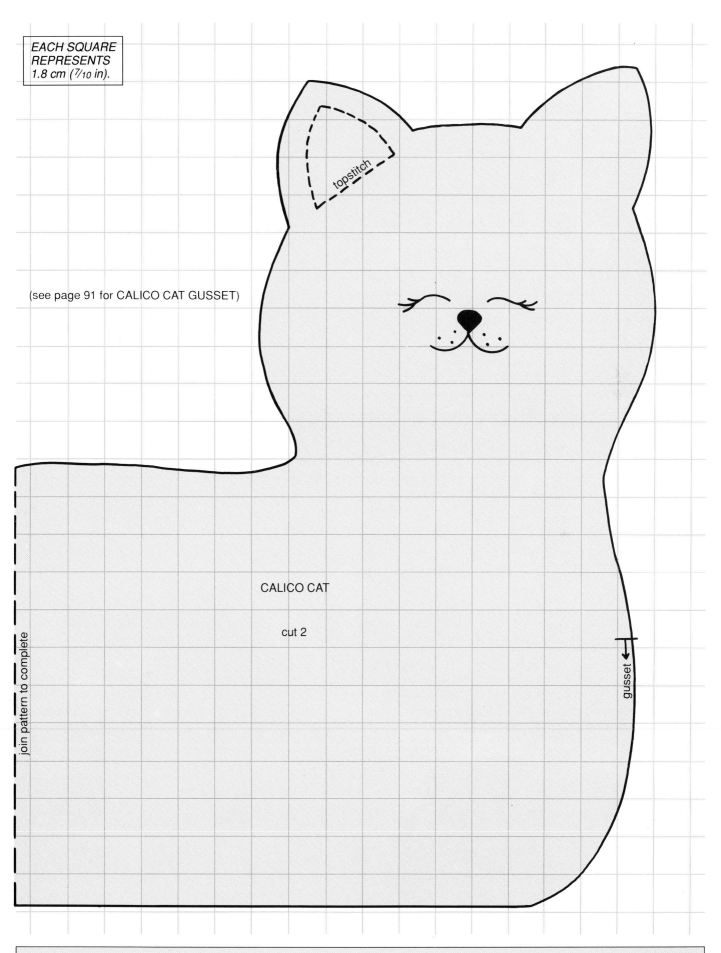

EACH SQUARE
REPRESENTS
1.8 cm (7/10 in).

topstitch

(see page 91 for CALICO CAT GUSSET)

CALICO CAT

cut 2

join pattern to complete

gusset

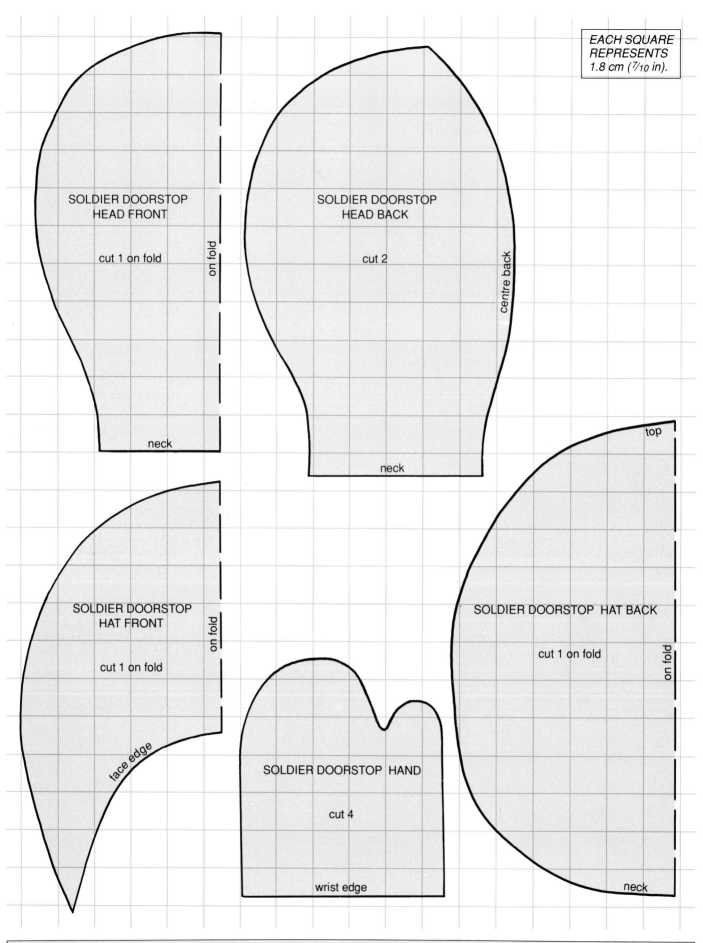

EACH SQUARE
REPRESENTS
1.8 cm (⁷/₁₀ in).

SOLDIER DOORSTOP
HEAD FRONT

cut 1 on fold

on fold

neck

SOLDIER DOORSTOP
HEAD BACK

cut 2

centre back

neck

SOLDIER DOORSTOP
HAT FRONT

cut 1 on fold

on fold

face edge

SOLDIER DOORSTOP HAND

cut 4

wrist edge

top

SOLDIER DOORSTOP HAT BACK

cut 1 on fold

on fold

neck

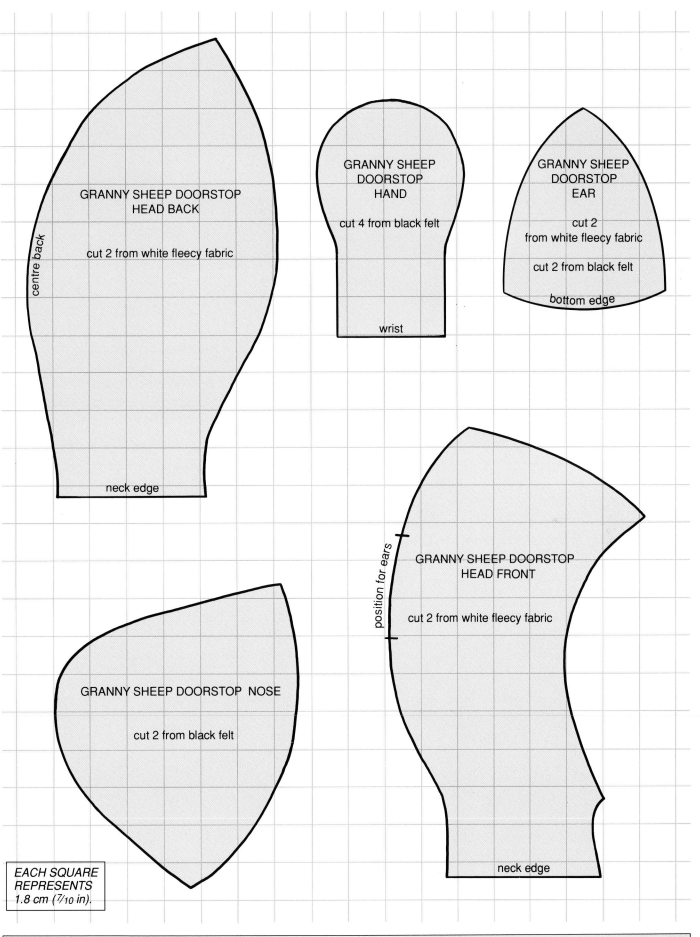

GRANNY SHEEP DOORSTOP
HEAD BACK

cut 2 from white fleecy fabric

centre back

neck edge

GRANNY SHEEP
DOORSTOP
HAND

cut 4 from black felt

wrist

GRANNY SHEEP
DOORSTOP
EAR

cut 2
from white fleecy fabric

cut 2 from black felt

bottom edge

GRANNY SHEEP DOORSTOP NOSE

cut 2 from black felt

GRANNY SHEEP DOORSTOP
HEAD FRONT

cut 2 from white fleecy fabric

position for ears

neck edge

EACH SQUARE
REPRESENTS
1.8 cm (7/10 in).

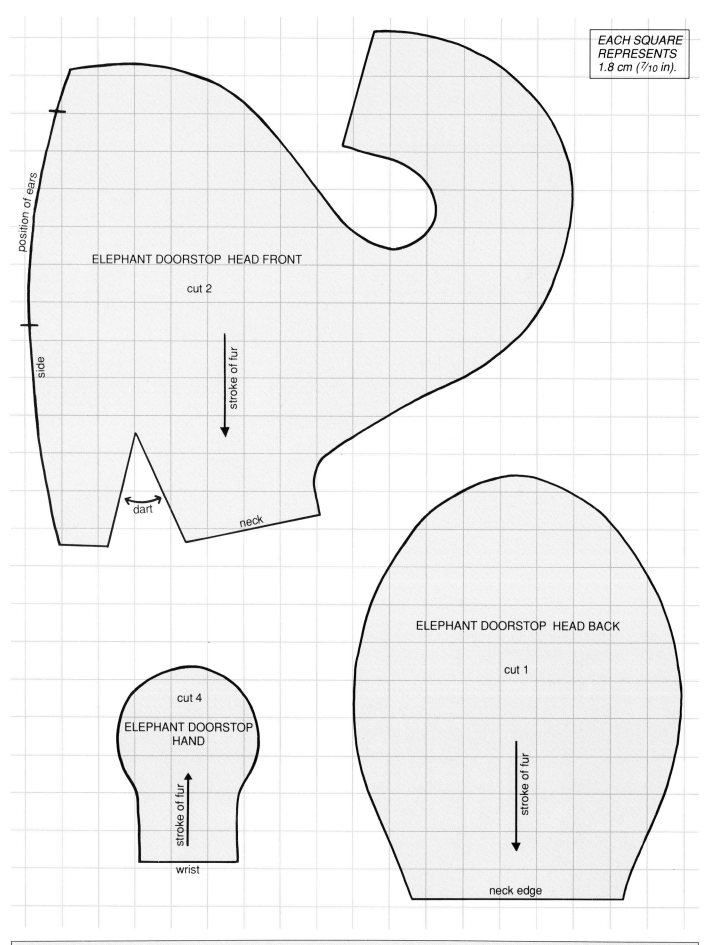

EACH SQUARE
REPRESENTS
1.8 cm (7/10 in).

position of ears

side

ELEPHANT DOORSTOP HEAD FRONT

cut 2

stroke of fur

dart

neck

ELEPHANT DOORSTOP HEAD BACK

cut 1

stroke of fur

cut 4
ELEPHANT DOORSTOP
HAND

stroke of fur

wrist

neck edge

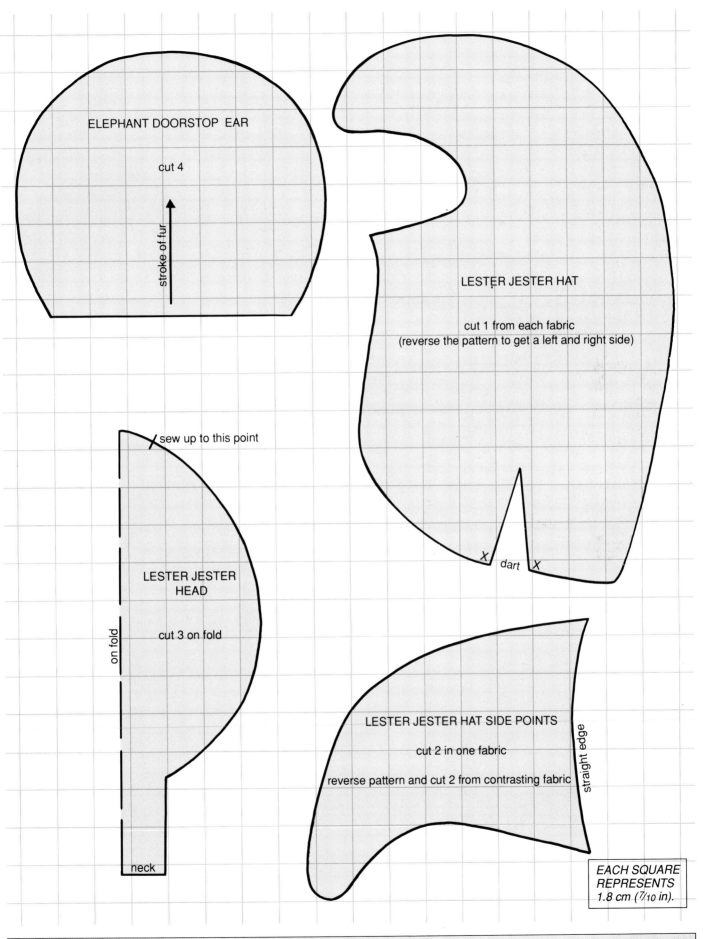

ELEPHANT DOORSTOP EAR

cut 4

stroke of fur

LESTER JESTER HAT

cut 1 from each fabric
(reverse the pattern to get a left and right side)

sew up to this point

LESTER JESTER
HEAD

cut 3 on fold

on fold

X   dart   X

neck

LESTER JESTER HAT SIDE POINTS

cut 2 in one fabric

reverse pattern and cut 2 from contrasting fabric

straight edge

EACH SQUARE
REPRESENTS
1.8 cm (⁷/₁₀ in).

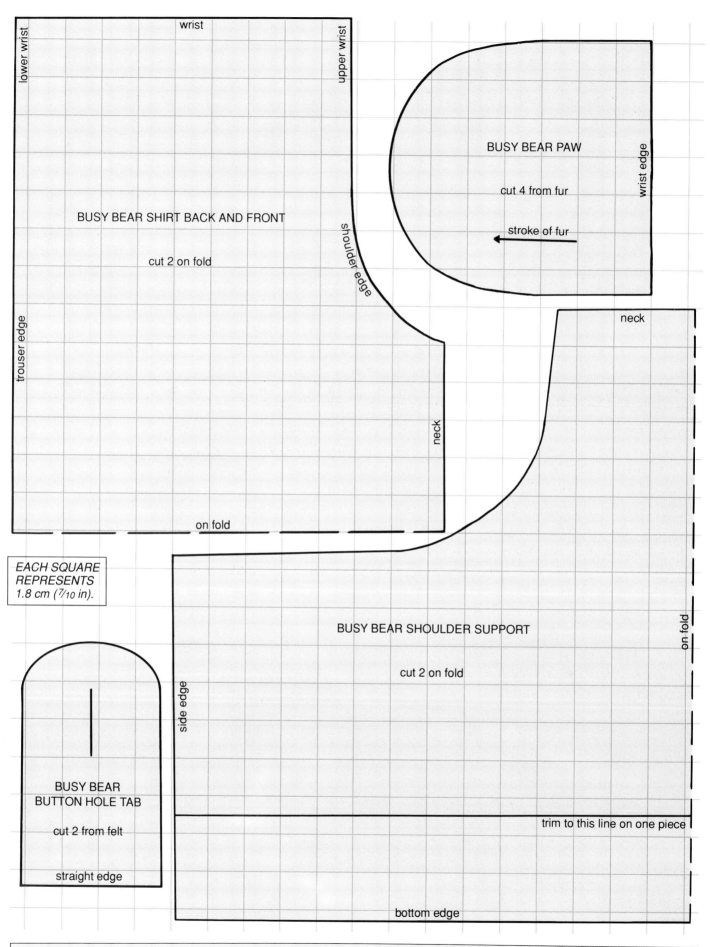

wrist

lower wrist

upper wrist

BUSY BEAR SHIRT BACK AND FRONT

cut 2 on fold

shoulder edge

trouser edge

neck

on fold

BUSY BEAR PAW

cut 4 from fur

stroke of fur

wrist edge

neck

on fold

EACH SQUARE
REPRESENTS
1.8 cm (7/10 in).

BUSY BEAR SHOULDER SUPPORT

cut 2 on fold

side edge

BUSY BEAR
BUTTON HOLE TAB

cut 2 from felt

straight edge

trim to this line on one piece

bottom edge

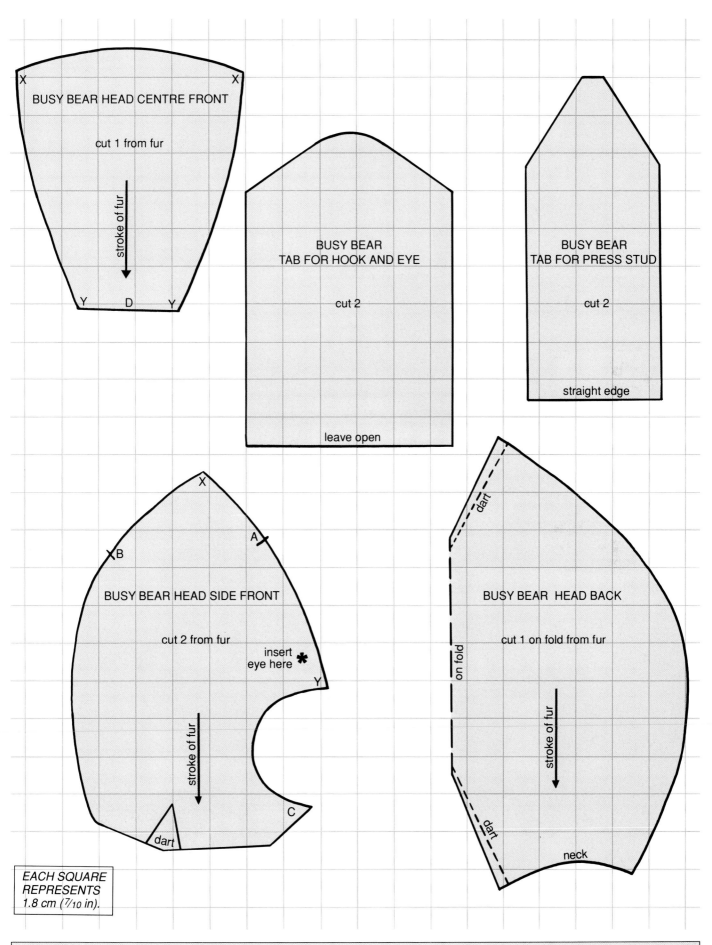

BUSY BEAR HEAD CENTRE FRONT

cut 1 from fur

stroke of fur

X   X

Y   D   Y

BUSY BEAR
TAB FOR HOOK AND EYE

cut 2

leave open

BUSY BEAR
TAB FOR PRESS STUD

cut 2

straight edge

BUSY BEAR HEAD SIDE FRONT

cut 2 from fur

insert
eye here ✻

stroke of fur

X

A

X B

Y

C

dart

BUSY BEAR HEAD BACK

cut 1 on fold from fur

dart

on fold

stroke of fur

dart

neck

EACH SQUARE
REPRESENTS
1.8 cm (⁷/10 in).

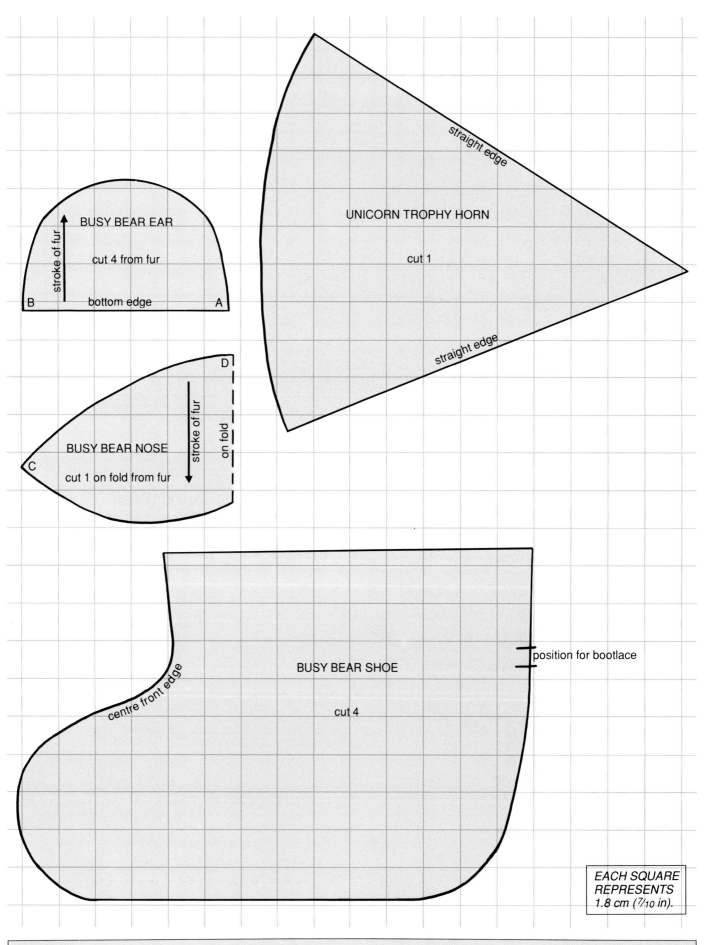

BUSY BEAR EAR

cut 4 from fur

stroke of fur

B   bottom edge   A

UNICORN TROPHY HORN

cut 1

straight edge

straight edge

D

BUSY BEAR NOSE

cut 1 on fold from fur

stroke of fur

on fold

C

BUSY BEAR SHOE

cut 4

centre front edge

position for bootlace

EACH SQUARE
REPRESENTS
1.8 cm (7/10 in).

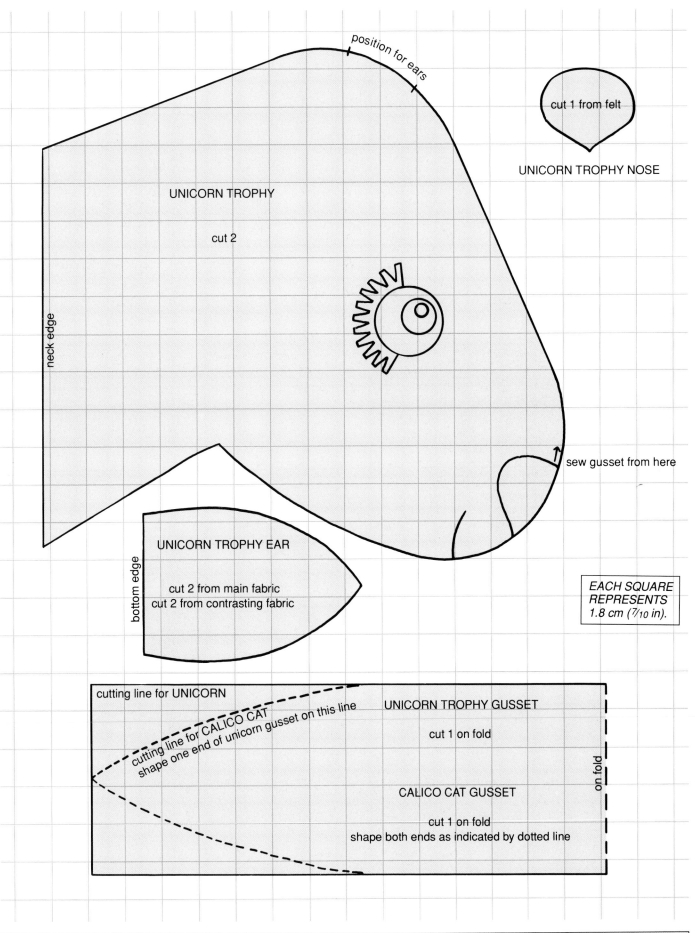

position for ears

cut 1 from felt

UNICORN TROPHY NOSE

UNICORN TROPHY

cut 2

neck edge

sew gusset from here

bottom edge

UNICORN TROPHY EAR

cut 2 from main fabric
cut 2 from contrasting fabric

EACH SQUARE
REPRESENTS
1.8 cm (⁷/₁₀ in).

cutting line for UNICORN

cutting line for CALICO CAT
shape one end of unicorn gusset on this line

UNICORN TROPHY GUSSET

cut 1 on fold

CALICO CAT GUSSET

cut 1 on fold
shape both ends as indicated by dotted line

on fold

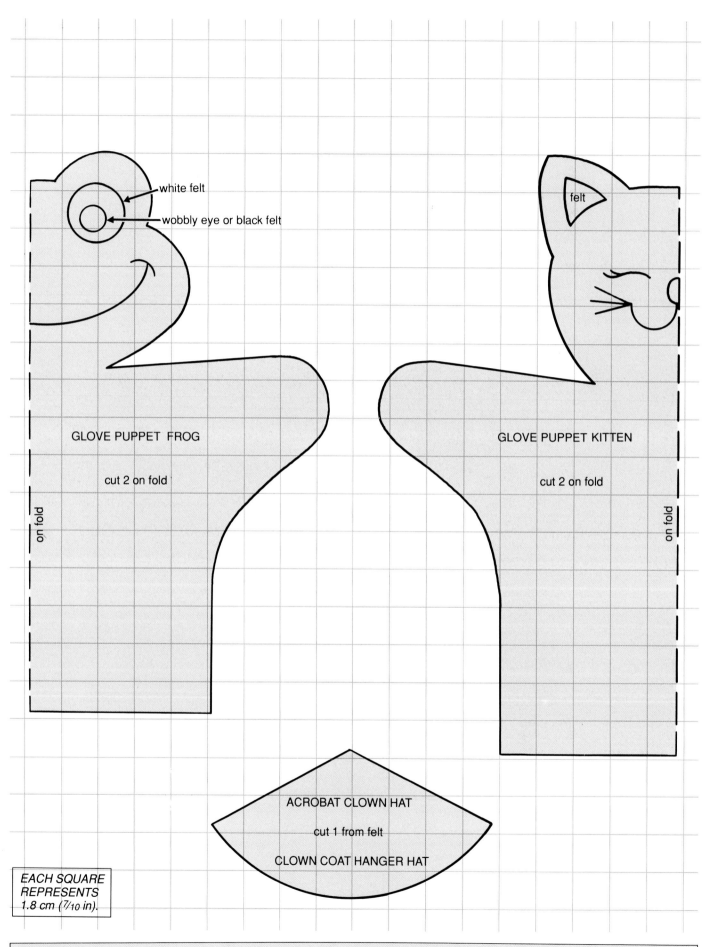

white felt

wobbly eye or black felt

felt

GLOVE PUPPET FROG

cut 2 on fold

on fold

GLOVE PUPPET KITTEN

cut 2 on fold

on fold

ACROBAT CLOWN HAT

cut 1 from felt

CLOWN COAT HANGER HAT

EACH SQUARE
REPRESENTS
1.8 cm (7/10 in).

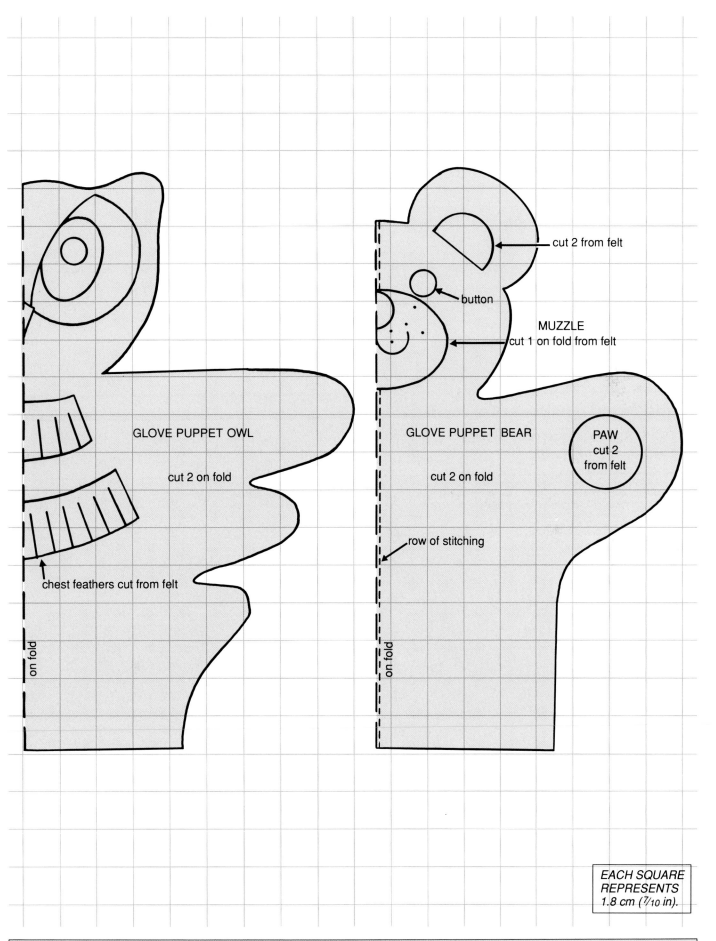

cut 2 from felt

button

MUZZLE
cut 1 on fold from felt

GLOVE PUPPET OWL

cut 2 on fold

GLOVE PUPPET BEAR

cut 2 on fold

PAW
cut 2
from felt

row of stitching

chest feathers cut from felt

on fold

on fold

*EACH SQUARE
REPRESENTS
1.8 cm (⁷/₁₀ in).*

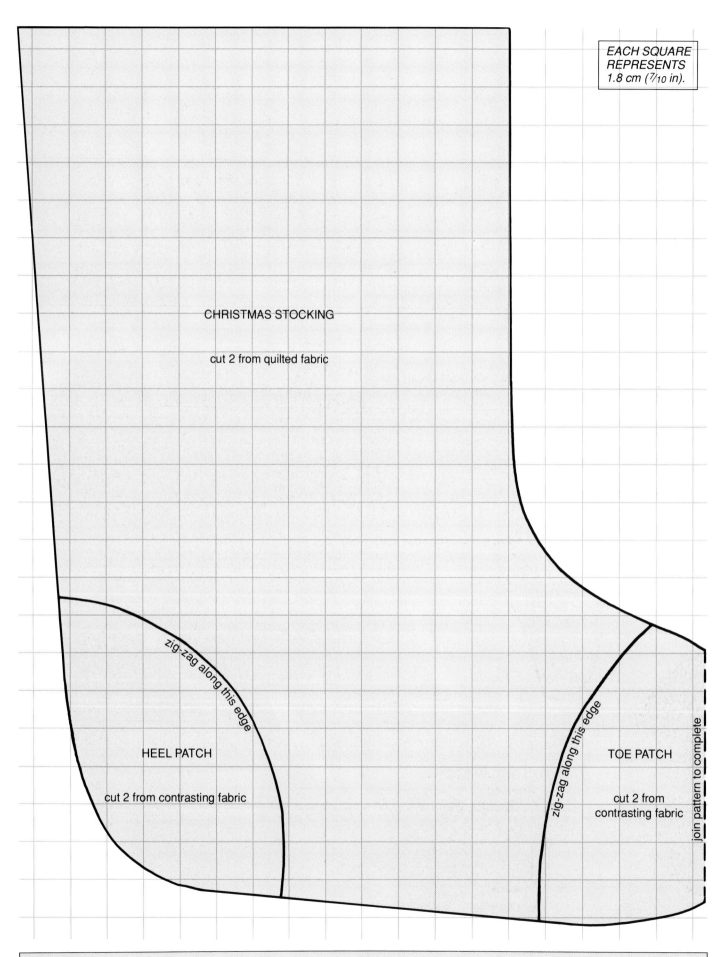

EACH SQUARE
REPRESENTS
1.8 cm (7/10 in).

CHRISTMAS STOCKING

cut 2 from quilted fabric

zig-zag along this edge

HEEL PATCH

cut 2 from contrasting fabric

zig-zag along this edge

TOE PATCH

cut 2 from
contrasting fabric

join pattern to complete

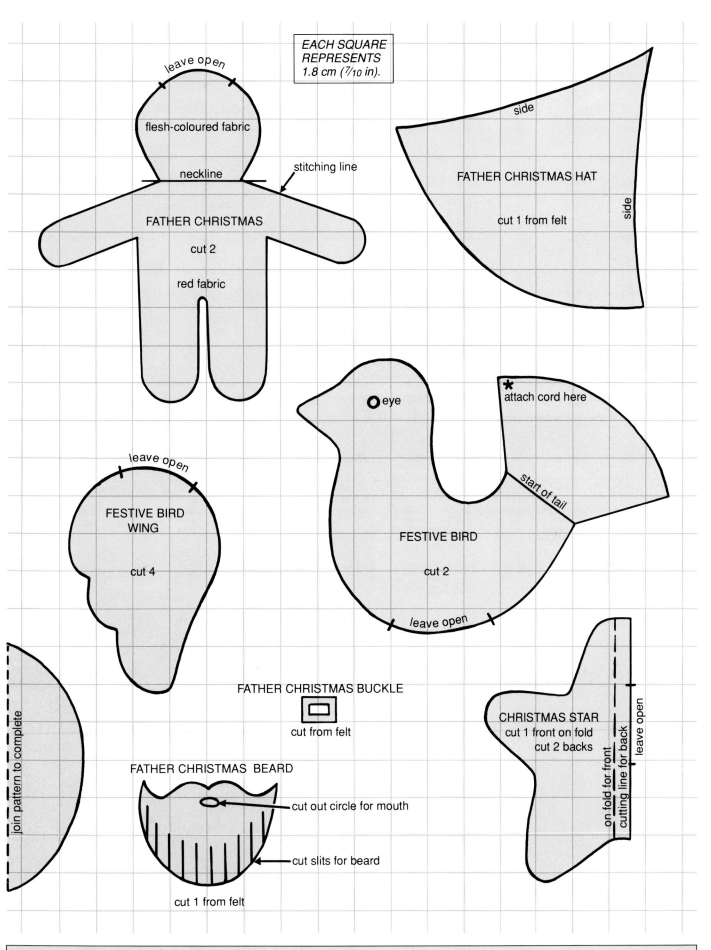

EACH SQUARE REPRESENTS 1.8 cm (⁷⁄₁₀ in).

leave open

flesh-coloured fabric

neckline

stitching line

FATHER CHRISTMAS

cut 2

red fabric

FATHER CHRISTMAS HAT

cut 1 from felt

side

side

eye

* attach cord here

start of tail

leave open

FESTIVE BIRD WING

cut 4

FESTIVE BIRD

cut 2

leave open

FATHER CHRISTMAS BUCKLE

cut from felt

CHRISTMAS STAR
cut 1 front on fold
cut 2 backs

on fold for front

cutting line for back

leave open

join pattern to complete

FATHER CHRISTMAS BEARD

cut out circle for mouth

cut slits for beard

cut 1 from felt